J.M. Barrie: Peter Pan
a new adaption by John Caird and Trevor Nunn

Sir James Barrie was born at Angus in Scotland in 1860, the son of a weaver. Educated at Dumfries Academy and Edinburgh University, his first career was that of a journalist, moving to London in 1884. He wrote a series of autobiographical novels, the best, *Margaret Ogilvy*, being an extraordinary portrait of his mother. He then turned his hand to plays, his first attempt, *Walker, London* in 1893 was an instant success. His other best known plays are *Quality Street* (1902), *The Admirable Crichton* (1902), and *What Every Woman Knows* (1908). But it is as the creator of *Peter Pan* that he will be chiefly remembered. He died in London in 1937.

John Caird and **Trevor Nunn** have worked together on three major adaptations for the theatre: Charles Dickens' *Nicholas Nickleby*, which they directed and adapted with the playwright David Edgar; *Les Misérables*, adapted and directed from Boublil and Schonberg's musical version of Victor Hugo's novel; and *Peter Pan*, first produced at the RSC in 1982, and now in this new version for the Royal National Theatre.

for Stephen

PETER PAN

OR

THE BOY WHO WOULD NOT GROW UP

A Fantasy in Five Acts

by
J.M. BARRIE

in a new version by
JOHN CAIRD & TREVOR NUNN

Methuen Drama

Methuen Drama

Published by A & C Black Publishers Limited
36 Soho Square
London W1D 3QY

3 5 7 9 10 8 6 4 2

First published in the United Kingdom in 1998 by
Methuen Publishing Limited
Reprinted in 2006 by Methuen Drama,
an imprint of A & C Black Publishers Limited

A CIP catalogue record for this book is available from the British Library

ISBN 10: 0 413 73550 8
ISBN 13: 978 0 413 73550 8

Typeset by Deltatype Ltd, Birkenhead, Merseyside

Contents

Introduction

This adaptation of J.M. Barrie's play was prepared for the Royal National Theatre production at the Olivier Theatre in 1997–8. An earlier but rather different version was performed by the Royal Shakespeare Company at the Barbican Theatre from 1982–1984. Both versions were conflated from the wealth of material left behind by J.M. Barrie at his death, and it may be interesting to students of the play, or indeed to anyone wishing to perform this version, to give a brief outline of the history of the work and of our process in selecting and editing the material.

There is no one single document called *Peter Pan*. Barrie wrote his first version of the play in 1903 for its premiere stage performance in the following year, but he only finally published it as a play-text in 1928. His reluctance to commit himself to a finished text was largely owing to the disappointment he felt in the productions of the play mounted before that date, and the limitations placed on his fantasy by the relatively primitive theatrical techniques of the age. But as he makes clear in his own introduction to the published text, Barrie was also strongly tied to the work emotionally and found it very difficult to let his story go. Indeed so fascinated was he by his own creation that he could scarcely stop writing it!

The 1928 play script is the basis for this edition, but we have also drawn from Barrie's 'Notes for a Fairy Play', 1903; the original script of *Peter Pan* entitled *Anon – A Play*, 1903; the prompt script of the first production in 1904; the

American version of 1905; the novel of 1911, which is certainly the most complete version of the story and the strongest evidence we have of the author's true fantasy; and the film scenario which he wrote for Paramount in 1920 – for Charlie Chaplin to play the title role – a most imaginative piece of screen writing which, alas, never reached the screen. The final scene in which Peter meets the grown-up Wendy is taken partly from the novel and partly from a long extra scene which Barrie wrote in 1907 entitled *An Afterthought*, and which was performed once only, on 22nd February 1908.

We have included a lot of new material from this vast reservoir of discoveries, but have left out much more. There is no room, for instance, for the scene in which Peter and Wendy turn all the posh promenaders in Hyde Park into Harlequins and Columbines, and where we once again meet Hook, now a cruel headmaster. He is again swallowed by the Crocodile, who has crawled up out of the Serpentine, and he disappears down the animal's throat, pathetically begging Peter to be allowed to take a pack of cards with him! Another scene has 'twenty beautiful mothers' showing up at the Darling house to claim their offspring, and being rejected by Peter for their bossiness, indifference or over-fastidiousness. There is an entirely unlikely marriage between Wendy and Tootles, and strangest of all, in one version of the final scene, Nana, twenty years on, has been stuffed and mounted as a rocking-horse dog for Wendy's daughter Jane. This macabre notion was, happily, rejected by Barrie almost as soon as he had written it!

We have made some significant alterations, the greatest of which is the introduction of a new character, the Storyteller, who is in fact the author himself. To a reader of the play, one of its most enjoyable ingredients is Barrie's unmistakable authorial tone. He tells the story of Peter Pan partly through dialogue and partly by means of his inimitable stage directions. In a whimsical, ambiguous and ironical manner he speaks here as clearly to adults as he does to children. Moreover, many of the play's complicated conceits are only comprehensible if Barrie's commentary can be heard in parallel with the voices of his characters. This device also allows us to prepare our audience with some essential background history of the Darling family in a brief prologue, and to extend the narratives at the end of the play to include Barrie's heartbreaking and heartwarming conclusion to Peter and Wendy's story.

One of Barrie's most bitter disappointments was the quickly established tradition of having an actress play the part of Peter. He had wanted a real little boy to play the part but the laws of the land forbade children being on stage after nine o'clock at night, so his wishes were confounded. He then tried to persuade his producer, Charles Frohmann, to cast Gerald du Maurier in the part, but he was overruled and the role was created by Nina Boucicault. Within a few years Barrie's wonderful fantasy had become what he most dreaded – a pantomime, as it is still most often played today. The problem remains. The part of Peter is, in fact, much too complex and emotionally challenging for any but the most gifted of children to perform successfully, but to allow a play about a boy and a girl to be acted out by two grown women is really most perverse. We solve the problem by casting all the children's roles with young adult actors and asking the audience to believe that they are children. Barrie instructs that 'all the characters whether grown ups, or babies, must wear a child's outlook on life as their only important adornment'. It is a short step from this statement to requiring a group of twenty-year-old actors to become a group of ten-year-old lost boys, and requiring an audience to join in the conspiracy!

And so they always will if the parts are played well enough and the audience is happy enough to believe in them. Most actors, young or old, find a return to their childhood surprisingly easy, and if the actors make the journey with sufficient belief, the audience is sure to follow.

One small, but apparently important, detail has been omitted from the 1928 script. In the nursery in Act One, Peter refuses to let Wendy touch him, and Barrie adds in a stage direction, 'He is never touched by anyone in the play'. This idea was never part of the author's original plan. It was added for Jean Forbes-Robertson's spiritual and Ariel-like performance in the late 1920s. We have left it out because of its inconsistency both with Peter's character and with the action of the play. Peter is required to touch members of his tribe on numerous occasions, some of them quite essential for the story to develop. More importantly, we felt that an audience should believe in Peter not as an airy sprite but as a thoroughly boyish little boy. There are fairies enough in Never Land without Peter adding to their number. Tinker Bell herself is an extremely physical and female example of one, conceived by Barrie as 'a girl exquisitely gowned in a skeleton leaf, cut low and square, through which her figure can be seen to best advantage. She was slightly inclined to *embonpoint*'. We have included some of her actual dialogue in the script, drawn from Barrie's own hints as well as guesses of our own. But whether Tink is aurally represented by a tinkling bell or, as in our production, with the added help of an ingenious electronic device, her words should never be entirely audible. It is only Peter, and of course her own fairy peers, who ever fully understand her language.

The Starkey/Smee front cloth scene between Acts Four and Five was written by Barrie in an awful hurry to cover a nasty scene change from the Never Land back to the Nursery.

It isn't terribly good and is eminently cuttable, but we needed it. If you can do without it, well done! But if you have a Never Land as complete and as beautiful as ours, and a Darling Home as perfect – both designed by our dear friend and colleague John Napier – you'll need the Starkey/Smee scene too!

Our single most important debt in the presentation of this edition is to Andrew Birkin, who first gave us access to all the source material, and guided us through it with an expert and friendly hand. His remarkable television series *The Lost Boys* movingly documents the relationship between J.M. Barrie and the Llewellyn-Davies family, the tie which first inspired his creation of the play. The research done for this series also forms the basis of Andrew Birkin's book *The Lost Boys*, published by Constable in 1979. For anyone who seeks to understand the genesis of the Peter Pan myth and the tragic story behind it, this is essential reading.

Perhaps the most revealing comment Barrie ever made on the character of Peter was in a programme note for the Paris production of 1908:

> Of Peter himself you must make what you will. Perhaps he was a little boy who died young, and this is how the author conceived his subsequent adventures. Perhaps he was a boy who was never born at all – a boy whom some people longed for, but who never came. It may be that those people hear him at the window more clearly than children do.

This remark was certainly, and most poignantly, true of Barrie himself and may go some way towards explaining his reluctance to publishing a final version of his child's adventures. We hope that the present edition remains faithful to the father's intentions and to the child's spirit, and that it will be as well appreciated by the lost parents of the Never Land as by their lost children.

Barrie's original dedication is included in this volume in full and it is, without question, to the five Llewellyn-Davies boys that the work owes its greatest inspiration. If we may be allowed our own dedication it is to the memory of our dear friend Stephen Oliver, whose ravishingly beautiful and haunting score is, we think, one of the most memorable features of our production. For this version it has been lovingly restored and expanded by his friend and colleague, Jonathan Dove. Stephen was a composer of real genius, and a Peter Pan himself, who piped melodies of great sweetness for all of his terribly short life. Stephen's music, just like Peter's, will play on, and on, till we wake up.

John Caird
Trevor Nunn

For those wishing to do their own production of this version

A Note on Design

We have not included in this text any description of John Napier's brilliant design for the Royal National Theatre production, it being of such a complexity and size that very few theatre companies could possibly afford to construct it, or indeed to give it house-room. In any event, there are many different possible design solutions for the play and no such thing as an unsuitable theatre for it. Wherever there is a stage, and an auditorium along with it, there *Peter Pan* can be performed. All you will need is a nursery with a window for Peter to fly in and for all the children to fly out, and a magical Never Land, fully described by Barrie in his stage direction at the beginning of Act Two, and which must be realised however you'd most like it to be! Perhaps the only rule in designing *Peter Pan* is that the director and designer should follow Barrie's advice to his actors – they 'must wear a child's outlook on life as their only important adornment'.

One word of warning. However you achieve your nursery and your Never Land, get your flying sorted out first! Don't design the show and then wonder how to do the flying. If you do, you will inevitably find yourselves flying into the scenery. You would, indeed, be well advised to consult a firm of experts – those ingenious professionals who alone fully understand the secrets of the fairy dust.

A Note on Music

We have not included Stephen Oliver's wonderful score in this publication of our version as there will no doubt be theatre companies who, for reasons of economy or artistry, will wish to use their own musical ideas. Stephen's music is available for rent to anyone who wants to use it and it can be ordered from Novello & Co. Ltd, Music Rental Library, Music Sales Distribution Centre, Newmarket Road, Bury St Edmunds, Suffolk IP33 3YP.

To the Five

A Dedication

Some disquising confessions must be made in printing at last
the play of *Peter Pan*; among them this, that I have no
recollection of having written it. Of that, however, anon.
What I want to do first is to give Peter to the Five without
whom he never would have existed. I hope, my dear sirs, that
in memory of what we have been to each other you will accept
this dedication with your friend's love. The play of Peter is
streaky with you still, though none may see this save
ourselves. A score of Acts had to be left out, and you were in
them all. We first brought Peter down, didn't we, with a
blunt-headed arrow in Kensington Cardens? I seem to
remember that we believed we had killed him, though he was
only winded, and that after a spasm of exultation in our
prowess the more soft-hearted among us wept and all of us
thought of the police. There was not one of you who would
not have sworn as an eye-witness to this occurrence; no doubt
I was abetting, but you used to provide corroboration that
was never given to you by me. As for myself, I suppose I
always knew that I made Peter by rubbing the five of you
violently together, as savages with two sticks produce a flame.
That is all he is, the spark I got from you.

We had good sport of him before we clipped him small
to make him fit the boards. Some of you were not born when
the story began and yet were hefty figures before we saw that
the game was up. Do you remember a garden at Burpham and

the initiation there of No. 4 when he was six weeks old, and three of you grudged letting him in so young? Have you No. 3, forgotten the white violets at the Cistercian abbey in which we cassocked our first fairies (all little friends of St Benedict), or your cry to the Gods, 'Do I just kill one pirate all the time?' Do you remember Marooners' Hut in the haunted groves of Waverley, and the St Bernard dog in a tiger's mask who so frequently attacked you, and the literary record of that summer, *The Boy Castaways*, which is so much the best and the rarest of this author's works? What was it that made us eventually give to the public in the thin form of a play that which had been woven for ourselves alone? Alas, I know what it was, I was losing my grip. One by one as you swung monkey-wise from branch to branch in the wood to make believe you reached the tree of knowledge. Sometimes you swung back into the wood, as the unthinking may at a cross-road take a familiar path that no longer leads to home; or you perched ostentatiously on its boughs to please me, pretending that you still belonged; soon you knew it only as the vanished wood, for it vanishes if one needs to look for it. A time came when I saw that No. 1, the most gallant of you all, ceased to believe that he was ploughing woods incarnadine and with an apologetic eye for me derided the lingering faith of No. 2; when even No. 3 questioned gloomily whether he did not really spend his nights in bed. There were still two who knew no better, but their day was dawning. In these circumstances, I suppose, was begun the writing of the play of Peter. That was a quarter of a century ago, and I clutch my brows in vain to remember whether it was a last desperate throw to retain the five of you for a little longer, or merely a cold decision to turn you into bread and butter.

This brings us back to my uncomfortable admission that I have no recollection of writing the play of *Peter Pan*, now being published for the first time so long after he made his bow upon the stage. You had played it until you tired of it, and tossed it in the air and gored it and left it derelict in the mud and went on your way singing other songs; and then I stole back and sewed some of the gory fragments together with a pen-nib. That is what must have happened, but I cannot remember doing it. I remember writing the story of *Peter and Wendy* many years after the production of the play, but I might have cribbed that from some typed copy. I can haul back to mind the writing of almost every other assay of mine, however forgotten by the pretty public; but this play of Peter, no. Even my beginning as an amateur playwright, that noble mouthful, *Bandelero the Bandit*, I remember every detail of its composition in my school days at Dumfries. Not less vivid is my first little piece, produced by Mr Toole. It was called *Ibsen's Ghost*, and was a parody of the mightiest craftsman that ever wrote for our kind friends in front. To save the management the cost of typing I wrote out the 'parts', after being told what parts were, and I can still recall my first words, spoken so plaintively by a now famous actress, – 'To run away from my second husband just as I ran away from my first, it feels quite like old times'. On the first night a man in the pit found *Ibsen's Ghost* so diverting that he had to be removed in hysterics. After that no one seems to have thought of it at all. But what a man to carry about with one! How odd, too, that these trifles should adhere to the mind that cannot remember the long job of writing Peter. It does seem almost suspicious, especially as I have not the original manuscript of *Peter Pan* (except a few stray pages) with which to support my claim. I have indeed another manuscript, lately made, but that 'proves nothing'. I know not whether I lost that original manuscript or destroyed it or happily gave it away. I talk of dedicating the play to you, but how can I prove it is mine? How ought I to act if some other hand, who could also have made a copy, thinks it worth while to contest the cold rights? Cold they are to me now as that laughter of yours in which Peter came into being long before he was caught and written down. There is Peter still, but to me he lies sunk in the gay Black Lake.

Any one of you five brothers has a better claim to the authorship than most, and I would not fight you for it, but you should have launched your case long ago in the days when you most admired me, which were in the first year of the play, owing to a rumour's reaching you that my spoils were one-and-sixpence a night. This was untrue, but it did give me a standing among you. You watched for my next play with peeled eyes, not for entertainment but lest it contained some chance witticism of yours that could be challenged as collaboration; indeed I believe there still exists a legal document, full of the Aforesaid and Henceforward to be called Part-Author, in which for some such snatching I was tied down to pay No. 2 one halfpenny daily throughout the run of the piece.

During the rehearsals of *Peter* (and it is evidence in my favour that I was admitted to them) a depressed man in overalls, carrying a mug of tea or a paint-pot, used often to appear by my side in the shadowy stalls and say to me, 'The gallery won't stand it'. He then mysteriously faded away as if he were the theatre ghost. This hopelessness of his is what all dramatists are said to feel at such times, so perhaps he was the author. Again, a large number of children whom I have seen playing Peter in their homes with careless mastership, constantly putting in better words, could have thrown it off with ease. It was for such as they that after the first production I had to add something to the play at the request of parents (who thus showed that they thought me the responsible person) about no one being able to fly until the fairy dust had been blown on him; so many children having gone home and tried it from their beds and needed surgical attention.

Notwithstanding other possibilities, I think I wrote Peter and if so it must have been in the usual inky way. Some of it, I like to think, was done in that native place which is the dearest spot on earth to me, though my last heart-beats shall be with my beloved solitary London that was so hard to reach. I must have sat at a table with that great dog waiting for me to stop, not complaining, for he knew it was thus we made our living, but giving me a look when he found he was to be in the play, with his sex changed. In after years when the actor who was Nana had to go to the wars he first taught his wife how to take his place as the dog till he came back, and I am glad that I see nothing funny in this; it seems to me to belong to the play. I offer this obtuseness on my part as my first proof that I am the author.

Some say that we are different people at different periods of our lives, changing not through effort of will, which is a brave affair, but in the easy course of nature every ten years or so. I suppose this theory might explain my present trouble, but I don't hold with it; I think one remains the same person throughout, merely passing, as it were, in these lapses of time from one room to another, but all in the same house. If we unlock the rooms of the far past we can peer in and see ourselves, busily occupied in beginning to become you and me. Thus, if I am the author in question the way he is to go should already be showing in the occupant of my first compartment, at whom I now take the liberty to peep. Here he is at the age of seven or so with his fellow-conspirator Robb, both in glengarry bonnets. They are giving an entertainment in a tiny old washing-house that still stands. The charge for admission is preens, a bool, or a peerie (I taught you a good deal of Scotch, so possibly you can follow that), and apparently the culminating Act consists in our trying to put each other into the boiler, though some say that I also addressed the spell-bound audience. This washing-house is not only the theatre of my first play, but has a still closer connection with Peter. It is the original of the little house the Lost Boys built in the Never Land for Wendy, the chief difference being that it never wore John's tall hat as a chimney. If Robb had owned a lum hat I have no doubt that it would have been placed on the washing-house.

Here is that boy again some four years older, and the reading he is munching feverishly is about desert islands; he calls them wrecked islands. He buys his sanguinary tales surreptitiously in penny numbers. I see a change coming over him; he is blanching as he reads in the high-class magazine, *Chatterbox*, a fulmination against such literature, and sees that unless his greed for islands is quenched he is for ever lost. With gloaming he steals out of the house, his library bulging beneath his palpitating waistcoat. I follow like his shadow, as indeed I am, and watch him dig a hole in a field at Pathhead farm and bury his islands in it; it was ages ago, but I could walk straight to that hole in the field now and delve for the remains. I peep into the next compartment. There he is again, ten years older, an under-graduate now and craving to be a real explorer, one of those who do things instead of prating of them, but otherwise unaltered; he might be painted at twenty on top of a mast, in his hand a spy-glass through which he rakes the horizon for an elusive strand. I go from room to room, and he is now a man, real exploration abandoned (though only because no one would have him). Soon he is even concocting other plays, and quaking a little lest some low person counts how many islands there are in them. I note that with the years the islands grow more sinister, but it is only because he has now to write with the left hand, the right having given out; evidently one thinks more darkly down the left arm. Go to the keyhole of the compartment where he and I join up, and you may see us wondering whether they would stand one more island. This journey through the house may not convince any one that I wrote Peter, but it does suggest me as as likely person. I pause to ask myself whether I read *Chatterbox* again, suffered the old agony, and buried the manuscript of the play in a hole in a field.

Of course this is over-charged. Perhaps we do change; except a little something in us which is no larger than a mote in the eye, and that, like it, dances in front of us beguiling us all our days. I cannot cut the hair by which it hangs.

The strongest evidence that I am the author is to be found, I think, in a now melancholy volume, the aforementioned *The Boy Castaways*; so you must excuse me for parading that work here. Officer of the Court, call *The Boy Castaways*. The witness steps forward and proves to be a book you remember well though you have not glanced at it these many years. I pulled it out of a bookcase just now not without difficulty, for its recent occupation has been to support the shelf above. I suppose, though I am uncertain, that it was I and not you who hammered it into that place of utility. It is a little battered and bent after the manner of those who shoulder burdens, and ought (to our shame) to remind us of the witnesses who sometimes get an hour off from the cells to give evidence before his Lordship. I have said that it is the rarest of my printed works, as it must be, for the only edition was limited to two copies, of which one (there was always some devilry in any matter connected with Peter) instantly lost itself in a railway carriage. This is the survivor. The idlers in court may have assumed that it is a handwritten screed, and are impressed by its bulk. It is printed by Constable's (how handsomely you did us, dear Blaikie), it contains thirty-five illustrations and is bound in cloth with a picture stamped on the cover of the three eldest of you 'setting out to be wrecked'. This record is supposed to be edited by the youngest of the three, and I must have granted him that honour to make up for his being so often lifted bodily out of our adventures by his nurse, who kept breaking into them for the fell purpose of giving him a midday rest. No. 4 rested so much at this period that he was merely an honourary member of the band, waving his foot to you for luck when you set off with bow and arrow to shoot his dinner for him; and one may rummage the book in vain for any trace of No. 5. Here is the title page except that you are numbered instead of named –

THE BOY
CASTAWAYS
OF BLACK LAKE ISLAND
being a record of the Terrible
Adventures of Three Brothers
in the summer of 1901
faithfully set forth
by No. 3.

LONDON
Published by J.M. Barrie
in the Gloucester Road
1901

There is a long preface by No. 3 in which we gather your ages at this first flight. 'No. 1 was eight and a month, No. 2 was approaching his seventh lustrum, and I was a good bit past four.' Of his two elders, while commending their fearless dispositions, the editor complains that they wanted to do all the shooting and carried the whole equipment of arrows inside their shirts. He is attractively modest about himself.

'Of No. 3 I prefer to say nothing, hoping that the tale as it is unwound will show that he was a boy of deeds rather than of words', a quality which he hints did not unduly protrude upon the brows of Nos. 1 and 2. His preface ends on a high note, 'I should say that the work was in the first instance compiled as a record simply at which we could whet our memories, and that it is now published for No. 4's benefit. If it teaches him by example lessons in fortitude and manly endurance we shall consider that we were not wrecked in vain'.

Published to whet your memories. Does it whet them? Do you hear once more, like some long-forgotten whistle beneath your window (Robb at dawn calling me to the fishing!) the not quite mortal blows that still echo in some of the chapter headings? – 'Chapter II, No. 1 teaches Wilkinson (his master) a Stern Lesson – We Run Away to Sea. Chapter III, A Fearful Hurricane – Wreck of the 'Anna Pink' – We Go Crazy from Want of Food – Proposal to eat No. 3 – Land Ahoy'. Such are two chapters out of sixteen. Are these again your javelins cutting tunes in the blue haze of the pines; do you sweat as you scale the dreadful Valley of Rolling Stones; and cleanse your hands of pirate blood by scouring them carelessly in Mother Earth? Can you still make a fire (you could do it once, Mr Seton-Thompson taught us in, surely an odd place, the Reform Club) by rubbing those sticks together? Was it the travail of hut-building that subsequently advised Peter to find a 'home under the ground'? The bottle and mugs in that lurid picture, 'Last night on the Island,' seem to suggest that you had changed from Lost Boys into pirates, which was probably also a tendency of Peter's. Listen again to our stolen saw-mill, man's proudest invention; when he made the saw-mill he beat the birds for music in a wood.

The illustrations (full-paged) in *The Boy Castaways* are

all photographs taken by myself; some of them indeed of phenomena that had to be invented afterwards, for you were always off doing the wrong things when I pressed the button. I see that we combined instruction with amusement; perhaps we had given our kingly work to that effect. How otherwise account for such wording to the pictures as these: 'It is undoubtedly', says No. 1 in a fir tree that is bearing unwonted fruit, recently tied to it, 'the *Cocos nucifera*, for observe the slender columns supporting the crown of leaves which fall with a grace that no art can imitate'. 'Truly', continues No. 1 under the same tree in another forest as he leans upon his trusty gun, 'though the perils of these happenings are great, yet would I rejoice to endure still greater privations to be thus rewarded by such wondrous studies of Nature'. He is soon back to the practical, however, 'recognising the Mango (*Magnifera indica*) by its lancet-shaped leaves and the cucumber-shaped fruit'. No. 1 was certainly the right sort of voyager to be wrecked with, though if my memory fails me not, No. 2, to whom these strutting observations were addressed, sometimes protested because none of them was given to him. No. 3 being the author is in surprisingly few of the pictures, but this, you may remember was because the lady already darkly referred to used to pluck him from our midst for his siesta at 12 o'clock, which was the hour that best suited the camera. With a skill on which he has never been complimented the photographer sometimes got No. 3 nominally included in a wild-life picture when he was really in a humdrum house kicking on the sofa. Thus in a scene representing Nos. 1 and 2 sitting scowling outside the hut it is untruly written that they scowled because 'their brother was within singing and playing on a barbaric instrument'. The music, the unseen No. 3 is represented as saying (obviously forestalling No. 1), 'is rude and to a cultured ear discordant, but the songs like those of the Arabs are full of poetic imagery'. He was perhaps allowed to say this sulkily on the sofa.

Though *The Boy Castaways* has sixteen chapter headings, there is no other letterpress; an absence which possible purchasers might complain of, though there are surely worse ways of writing a book than this. These headings anticipate much of the play of *Peter Pan*, but there were many incidents of our Kensington Gardens days that never got into the book, such as our Antarctic exploits when we reached the Pole in advance of our friend Captain Scott and cut our initials on it for him to find, a strange foreshadowing of what was really to happen. In *The Boy Castaways* Captain Hook has arrived but is called Captain Swarthy, and he seems from the pictures to have been a black man. This character, as you do not need to be told, is held by those in the know to be autobiographical. You had many tussles with him (though you never, I think, got his right arm) before you reached the terrible chapter (which might be taken from the play) entitled 'We Board the Pirate Ship at Dawn – A Rakish Craft – No. 1 Hewthem-Down and No. 2 of the Red Hatchet – A Holocaust of Pirates – Rescue of Peter.' (Hullo, Peter rescued instead of rescuing others? I know what that means and so do you, but we are not going to give away all our secrets.) The scene of the Holocaust is the Black Lake (afterwards, when we let women in, the Mermaids' Lagoon). The pirate captain's end was not in the mouth of a Crocodile though we had Crocodiles on the spot ('while No. 2 was removing the Crocodiles from the stream No. 1 shot a few parrots, *Psittacidae*, for our evening meal'). I think our captain had divers deaths owing to unseemly competition among you, each wanting to slay him single-handed. On a special occasion, such as when No. 3 pulled out the tooth himself, you gave the deed to him, but took it from him while he rested. The only pictorial representation in the book of Swarthy's fate is in two parts. In one, called briefly 'We string him up'. Nos. 1 and 2, stern as Athos, are hauling him up a tree by a rope, his face snarling as if it were a grinning mask (which indeed it was), and his garments very like some of my own stuffed with bracken. The other, the same scene next day, is called 'The Vultures had Picked him Clean', and tells its own tale.

The dog in *The Boy Castaways* seems never to have been called Nana but was evidently in training for that post. He originally belonged to Swarthy (or to Captain Marryat?), and the first picture of him, lean, skulking, and hunched (how did I get that effect?), 'patrolling the island' in that monster's interests, gives little indication of the domestic paragon he was to become. We lured him away to the better life, and there is, later, a touching picture, a clear forecast of the Darling nursery, entitled 'We trained the dog to watch over us while we slept'. In this he also is sleeping, in a position that is a careful copy of his charges; indeed any trouble we had with him was because, once he knew he was in the story, he thought his safest course was to imitate you in everything you did. How anxious he was to show that he understood the game, and more generous than you, he never pretended that he was the one who killed Captain Swarthy. I must not imply that he was entirely without initiative, for it was his own idea to bark warningly a minute or two before twelve o'clock as a signal to No. 3 that his keeper was probably on her way for him (Disappearance of No. 3); and he became so used to living in the world of Pretend that when we reached the hut of a morning he was often there waiting for us, looking, it is true, rather idiotic, but with a new bark he had invented which puzzled as until we decided that he was demanding the password. He was always willing to do any extra jobs, such as becoming the tiger in mask, and when after fierce engagement you carried home that mask in triumph, he joined in the procession proudly and never let on that the trophy had ever been part of him. Long afterwards he saw the play from a box in the theatre, and as familiar scenes were unrolled before his eyes I have never seen a dog so bothered. At one matinee we even let him for a moment take the place of the actor who played Nana, and I don't know that any members of the audience ever noticed the change, though he introduced some 'business' that was new to them but old to you and me. Heigh-ho, I suspect that in this reminiscence I am mixing him up with his successor, for such a one there had to be, the loyal Newfoundland who, perhaps in the following year, applied, so to say, for the part by bringing hedgehogs to the hut in his mouth as offerings for our evening repasts. The head and coat of him were copied for the Nana of the play.

They do seem to be emerging out of our island, don't they, the little people of the play, all except that sly one, the chief figure, who draws farther and farther into the wood as we advance upon him? He so dislikes being tracked, as if there were something odd about him, that when he dies he means to get up and blow away the particles that will be his ashes.

Wendy has not yet appeared, but she has been trying to come ever since that loyal nurse cast the humorous shadow of woman upon the scene and made us feel that it might be fun to let in a disturbing element. Perhaps she would have bored her way in at last whether we wanted her or not. It may be that even Peter did not really bring her to the Never Land of his free will, but merely pretended to do so because she would not stay away. Even Tinker Bell had reached our island before we left it. It was one evening when we climbed the wood carrying No. 4 to show him what the trail was like by twilight. As our lanterns twinkled among the leaves No. 4 saw twinkle stand still for a moment and he waved his foot gaily to it, thus creating Tink. It must not be thought, however, that there were any other sentimental passages betweeen No. 4 and Tink; indeed, as he got to know her better he suspected her of frequenting the hut to see what we had been having for supper, and to partake of the same, and he pursued her with malignancy.

A safe but something chilly way of recalling the past is to force open a crammed drawer. If you are searching for anything in particular you don't find it, but something falls out at the back that is often more interesting. It is in this way that I get my desultory reading, which includes a few stray leaves of the original manuscript of Peter that I have said I do possess, though even they, when returned to the drawer, are gone again, as if that touch of devilry lurked in them still. They show that in early days I hacked at and added to the play. In the drawer I find some scraps of Mr Crook's delightful music, and other incomplete matter relating to Peter. Here is the reply of a boy whom I favoured with a seat in my box and injudiciously asked at the end what he had liked best. 'What I think I liked best', he said, 'was tearing up the programme and dropping the bits on people's heads'. Thus am I often laid low. A copy of my favourite programme of the play is still in the drawer. In the first or second year of Peter, No. 4 could not attend through illness, so we took the play to his nursery, far away in the country, an array of vehicles almost as glorious as a travelling circus; the leading parts were played by the youngest children in the London company, and No. 4, aged five, looked on solemnly at the performance from his bed and never smiled once. That was my first and only appearance on the real stage, and this copy of the programme shows I was thought so meanly of as an actor that they printed my name in smaller letters than the others.

I have said little here of Nos. 4 and 5, and it is high time I had finished. They had a long summer day, and I turn round twice and now they are off to school. On Monday, as it seems, I was escorting No. 5 to a children's party and brushing his hair in the ante-room; and by Thursday he is placing me against the wall of an underground station and saying, 'Now I am going to get the tickets; don't move till I come back for you or you'll lose yourself'. No. 4 jumps from being astride my shoulders fishing, I knee-deep in the stream, to becoming, while still a schoolboy, the sternest of my literary critics. Anything he shook his head over I abandoned, and conceivably the world has thus been deprived of masterpieces. There was for instance an unfortunate little tragedy which I liked until I foolishly told No. 4 its subject, when he frowned and said he had better have a look at it. He read it, and then, patting me on the back, as only he and No. 1 could touch me, said, 'You know you can't do this sort of thing'. End of a tragedian. Sometimes, however, No. 4 liked my efforts, and I walked in the azure that day when he returned *Dear Brutus* to me with the comment 'Not so bad'. In earlier days, when he was ten, I offered him the manuscript of my book *Margaret Ogilvy*. 'Oh, thanks', he said almost immediately, and added, 'Of course my desk is awfully full'. I reminded him that he could take out some of its more ridiculous contents. He said 'I have read it already in the book'. This I had not known, and I was secretly elated, but I said that people sometimes liked to preserve this kind of thing as a curiosity. He said 'Oh' again. I said tartly that he was not compelled to take it if he didn't want it. He said 'Of course I want it, but my desk –'. Then he wriggled out of the room and came back in a few minutes dragging in No. 5 and announcing triumphantly, 'No. 5 will have it'.

The rebuffs I have got from all of you! They were especially crushing in those early days when one by one you came out of your belief in fairies and lowered on me as the deceiver. My grandest triumph, the best thing in the play of *Peter Pan* (though it is not in it) is that long after No. 4 had ceased to believe, I brought him back to the faith for at least two minutes. We were on our way in a boat to fish the Outer Hebrides (where we caught *Mary Rose*), and though it was a journey of days he wore his fishing basket on his back all the time, so as to be able to begin at once. His one pain was the absence of Johnny Mackay, for Johnny was the loved gillie of the previous summer who had taught him everything that is worth knowing (which is a matter of flies) but could not be with us this time as he would have had to cross and re-cross Scotland to reach us. As the boat drew near the Kyle of Lochalsh pier I told Nos. 4 and 5 it was such a famous wishing pier, that they had now but to wish and they should have. No. 5 believed at once and expressed a wish to meet himself (I afterwards found him on the pier searching faces confidently), but No. 4 thought it more of my untimely nonsense and doggedly declined to humour me. 'Whom do you want to see most, No. 4?', 'Of course I would like most to see Johnny Mackay'. 'Well, then, wish for him.' 'Oh, rot,' 'It can't do any harm to wish.' Contemptuously he wished, and as the ropes were thrown on the pier he saw Johnny waiting for him, loaded with angling paraphernalia. I know no one less like a fairy than Johnny Mackay, but for two minutes No. 4 was quivering in another world than ours. When he came to he gave me a smile which meant that we understood each other, and thereafter neglected me for a month, being always with Johnny. As I have said, this episode is not in the play; so though I dedicate *Peter Pan* to you I keep the smile, with the few other broken fragments of immortality that have come my way.

J.M. Barrie

PETER PAN

OR

THE BOY WHO WOULD NOT GROW UP

This version of *Peter Pan* was first performed in the Olivier auditorium of the Royal National Theatre, London, on 16 December 1997. The cast was as follows:

The Storyteller	Alec McCowan
Mr Darling	Ian McKellen
Mrs Darling	Jenny Agutter
Wendy	Claudie Blakely
John	Adrian Ross-Magenty
Michael	Daniel Hart
Nana	Jan Knightly
Liza	Liza Hayden
Peter Pan	Daniel Evans
Tinker Bell	Sally-Ann Burnett
Slightly	Daniel Coonan
Tootles	Wayne Cater
Nibs	Harold Finlay
Curly	Johnny Hoskins
First Twin	Mark Channon
Second Twin	Dominic McHale
Ostrich	Simon Penman
Cecco	Anthony Venditti
Bill Jukes	Liam McKenna
Cookson	Michael Mawby
Gentleman Starkey	Bryan Robson
Chay Turley	Jim Creighton
Robert Mullins	Robert Aldous
Noodler	Jan Knightly
Skylights	Patrick Romer
Canary Robb	Ben Mangham
Wibbles	Murray MacArthur
Alsatian Fogarty	Simon Penman
Capt. James Hook	Ian McKellen

Smee	Clive Rowe
Great Big Little Panther	Murray MacArthur
Tiger Lily	Natalie Tinn
Piccaninny Tribe	Michelle Abrahams
	Sally-Ann Burnett
	Naomi Capron
	Jim Creighton
	Liza Hayden
	Ben Mangham
	Simon Penman
Mermaids	Michelle Abrahams
	Sally-Ann Burnett
	Naomi Capron
	Liza Hayden
Never Bird	Jenny Agutter
Jane	Michelle Abrahams

Directed by John Caird *with* Fiona Laird
Settings by John Napier
Costumes by Andreane Neofitou
Lighting by David Hersey
Music and additional lyrics by Stephen Oliver *arranged by*
Jonathan Dove

PROLOGUE

Music. Darkness. A match is lit, and a light comes up on the
STORYTELLER, *a slight man, impeccably attired in Edwardian dress. He is lighting a pipe. He turns, noticing the audience.*

Storyteller All children grow up ... except one. (*He thinks for a moment*) Have you ever seen a map of a child's mind? Doctors sometimes draw maps of other parts of you, but catch them trying to draw a map of a child's mind, which is not only confused, but keeps going round all the time. If you ever did see a map like that, you would be looking at a map of the Never Land ... with astonishing splashes of colour here and there, and coral reefs, and rakish looking craft in the offing, and savages, and lonely lairs, and gnomes who are mostly tailors, and princes with six elder brothers, and one very small old lady with a hooked nose.

On these magic shores, children at play are forever beaching their coracles. We grown-ups have been there. We can still hear the sound of the surf, though we shall never land there any more.

All children grow up ... except one! Peter Pan! The boy who *wouldn't* grow up.

The music tries to assert itself but the STORYTELLER *waves it away and continues with the story.*

I'll tell you.

MRS DARLING *drifts on from upstage and dreamily circles the* STORYTELLER.

Storyteller There never was a simpler, happier family than the Darling family. Mrs Darling was a lovely lady with a romantic mind and a sweet mocking mouth, which had one kiss on it that nobody could ever get.

He exchanges a little look with MRS DARLING *as* MR DARLING *appears at the side of the stage.*

The way Mr Darling won her was this. The many gentlemen who had been boys when she was a girl discovered simultaneously that they loved her, and they all ran up to her house to propose to her ... except Mr Darling ...

Mr Darling (*briskly crossing to* MRS DARLING) ... who took a cab and nipped in first!

Storyteller And so he got her.

Mrs Darling He got all of her.

Storyteller (*with great regret*) Except that kiss.

Mr Darling/Mrs Darling Mr and Mrs Darling had three children.

WENDY, JOHN *and* MICHAEL *run on to join their parents.*

Wendy Wendy came first!

John And then John!

Michael And then Michael!

Mrs Darling Mrs Darling loved to have everything just so . . .

Mrs Darling . . . and Mr Darling had a passion for being exactly like the neighbours . . .

Storyteller . . . so, of course, they had to have a nanny for the children.

Mrs Darling But as they were so poor . . .

Wendy . . . owing to the amount of milk the children drank . . .

Storyteller . . . their nanny was a very large dog called . . .

Michael Nana!

NANA *comes bounding on, knocking the* CHILDREN *over, and barking happily.*

All The Darlings Nana!

Storyteller Nana was trained by Mrs Darling.

Mrs Darling But like all treasures she was born to it.

MRS DARLING *puts an umbrella in* NANA's *mouth, and* NANA *turns on the* CHILDREN, *glaring them into line. The* CHILDREN *march off in single file, like soldiers, with* NANA *bringing up the rear, ready to butt them back into line if they stray.*

Storyteller Their only other servant was Liza.

LIZA *enters. She is so small that when she says she will never see ten again one can scarcely believe her. She carries a bucket and swab-cloth and sets to polishing the floor with it.*

Storyteller Such a midget she looked in her long skirt and maid's cap . . .

Mrs Darling . . . and somehow the Darlings had got into the way of calling her . . .

Everyone . . . 'the servants'.

Music. The whole FAMILY *dances,* NANA *included.*

Storyteller They all had lovely dances, and sometimes Liza was allowed to join in.

JOHN *dances with* LIZA *as* MRS DARLING *starts to spin at the centre of the stage.*

Storyteller The gaiety of those romps! And the gayest of all was Mrs Darling, who would pirouette so wildly that all you could see of her was . . . the kiss.

MRS DARLING's *spin ends in a mysterious smile as she exchanges another little glance of conspiracy with the* STORY-TELLER. *The* DARLINGS *start to leave the stage.*

Storyteller There never was a simpler, happier family, until the coming of Peter Pan.

MRS DARLING *turns back for a moment, almost as if she recalls the sound of that name, but can't quite place where she has heard it.* MR DARLING *takes her arm and they leave the stage.*

Storyteller They lived at Number 14 in a rather depressed street in Bloomsbury.

We have a right to place the house where we will, and the reason Bloomsbury is chosen is that Mr Roget once lived there. So did we in days when his thesaurus was our only companion in London; and we whom he has helped to wend our way through life have always wanted to pay him a little compliment. The Darlings therefore live in Bloomsbury.

It is a corner house whose top window, the important one, looks upon a leafy square from which Peter used to fly up to it, to the delight of three children and, no doubt, the irritation of passers-by. The street is still there, though the steaming sausage shop has gone; and apparently the same cards perch now as then over the doors, inviting homeless ones to come and stay with the hospitable inhabitants. Since the days of the Darlings, however, a lick of paint has been applied; and our corner house in particular, which has swallowed its neighbour, blooms with an awful freshness as if the colours had been discharged upon it with a hose. Its card now says 'no children', meaning maybe that the goings-on of Wendy and her brothers have given the house a bad name. As for ourselves we have not been in it since we went back to reclaim our old thesaurus.

The Darling house appears upstage.

Storyteller This is what we call the Darling house, but you may dump it down anywhere you like, and if you think it was your house you are very probably right. It wanders about London looking for anybody in need of it.

The house, or that part of it that is the nursery, wanders downstage and presents itself to the audience.

ACT ONE

The Nursery

Storyteller (*walking round the room he is describing*) The scene of our opening act is the night-nursery of the Darling family, a shabby little room if Mrs Darling had not made it the hub of creation by her certainty that such it was, and adorned it to match with a loving heart and all the scrapings of her purse.

The door on the right leads into the day-nursery, which she has no right to have, but she made it herself with nails in her mouth and a paste-pot in her hand. This is the door the children will come in by. There are three beds and a large dog-kennel; two of these beds, with the kennel, being on the left and the other on the right. Over each bed is a china house, the size of a linnet's nest, containing a night-light.

The coverlets of the beds are made out of her wedding gown. Supporting the mantelshelf are two soldiers, home-made, begun by Mr Darling, finished by Mrs Darling, repainted – unfortunately – by John Darling.

On the fireguard hang incomplete parts of children's night attire. The door on the left leads to the bathroom. In the centre is the window, which is at present ever so staid and respectable, but half an hour hence will be able to tell a very strange tale to the police.

It was the spring of the year. Wendy was already nearly twelve by now, John was ten and Michael was still so small that he spent most of his time doing idiotic things with a teddy bear. The only occupant of the room at present is Nana. The cuckoo-clock strikes six . . .

As the clock starts to strike, the STORYTELLER quietly leaves the stage, and NANA springs into life. This first moment in the play is tremendously important, for if the actor playing NANA does not spring properly we are undone. She will probably be played by a boy, if one clever enough can be found, and must never be on two legs except on those rare occasions when an ordinary nurse would be on four. The NANA must go about all her duties in a most ordinary manner so that you know in your bones that she performs them just so every evening at six; naturalness must be her passion; indeed it should be the aim of everyone in the play, for which she is now setting the pace. All the characters, whether grown-ups or babes, must wear a child's outlook on life as their only important adornment. If they cannot help being funny they are begged to go away. A good motto for all would be 'the little less, and how much it is'. NANA, making much use of her mouth, 'turns down' the beds, and carries the various articles on the fireguard across to them. MICHAEL enters and NANA barks at him.

Michael (*obstreperous*) I won't go to bed, I won't. Nana, it isn't six o'clock yet. Two minutes more, *please*. Nana, I won't be bathed, I tell you I will not be bathed.

NANA growls threateningly.

Michael Well, I won't have my head washed!

Here the bathroom door closes on them, and MRS DAR-LING, who has perhaps heard his cry, enters the nursery. As she is going out to dinner tonight she is already wearing her evening gown because she knows her children like to see her in it. It is a delicious confection made by herself out of nothing and other people's mistakes. She does not often go out to dinner, preferring when the children are in bed to sit beside them tidying up their minds, just as if they were drawers. If Wendy and the boys could keep awake they might just see her repacking into their proper places the many articles of the mind that have strayed during the day, lingering humorously over some of their contents, wondering where on earth they picked this thing up, making discoveries sweet and not so sweet, pressing this to her cheek and hurriedly stowing that out of sight. When they wake in the morning the naughtinesses with which they went to bed are not, alas, blown away, but they are placed at the bottom of the drawer; and on the top, beautifully aired, are their prettier thoughts ready for the new day. As she enters the room she is startled to see a strange little face outside the window and a hand groping as if it wanted to come in.

Mrs Darling (*whispering*) Who are you?

The unknown disappears; she hurries to the window.

No one there. And yet I feel sure I saw a face. (*A sudden awful thought*) My children!

She throws open the bathroom door and MICHAEL's *head appears gaily over the bath. He splashes and giggles; she throws kisses to him and closes the door.*

Mrs Darling Wendy! John!

Wendy Coming!

John 'Oh, this is too bad!'

MRS DARLING *sits down, relieved, on Wendy's bed.*

WENDY *and* JOHN *come in, looking their smallest size, as children tend to do to a mother suddenly in fear for them.*

John (*histrionically*) We are doing an act; we are playing at being you and Father.

He imitates the only father who has come under his special notice.

'A little less noise there.'

Wendy Now let us pretend we have a baby.

WENDY *hops in to her bed and prepares to receive the precious parcel.*

John I am happy to inform you, Mrs Darling, that you are now a mother.

WENDY *gives way to ecstasy.*

John You have missed the chief thing; you haven't asked, 'boy or girl?'

Wendy I am so glad to have one at all, I don't care which it is.

John (*crushingly*) That is just the difference between gentlemen and ladies. Now you tell me.

JOHN *and* WENDY *change places.*

Wendy I am happy to *acquaint* you, Mr Darling, you are now a father.

John Boy or girl?

Wendy (*presenting herself*) Girl!

John Tsk!

Wendy You horrid.

John Go on.

Wendy I am happy to acquaint you, Mr Darling, you are again a father.

John Boy or girl?

Wendy Boy.

JOHN *beams.*

Wendy Mummy, it's hateful of him.

MICHAEL *has been witnessing this little drama through a crack in the bathroom door and is now butted back into the nursery by* NANA. *He is wearing a set of John's old all-in-one pyjamas.*

Michael (*expanding*) Now, John, have me.

John We don't want any more.

Michael (*contracting*) Am I not to be born at all?

John Two is enough.

Michael (*wheedling*) Come, John. *Boy*, John.

JOHN *is implacable,* MICHAEL *appalled.*

Michael Nobody wants me!

Mrs Darling I do.

Michael (*with a glimmer of hope*) Boy or girl?

Mrs Darling (*with one of those happy thoughts of hers*) Boy!

Triumph of MICHAEL; *discomfiture of* JOHN. MR DARLING *arrives, in no mood, unfortunately, to gloat over this domestic scene. He is really a good man as breadwinners go and it is hard luck for him to be propelled into the room now, where if we had brought him in a few minutes earlier or later he might have made a fairer impression. In the city where he sits on a stool all day, as fixed as a postage stamp, he is so like all the others on stools that you recognize him not by his face but by his stool, but at home the way to gratify him is to say that he has a distinct personality. He is very conscientious, and in the days when Mrs Darling gave up keeping the house books correctly and drew pictures instead (which he called her guesses) he did all the totting up for her, holding her hand while he calculated whether they could have Wendy or not, and coming down on the right side. It is with regret, therefore, that we introduce him as a tornado, rushing into the nursery in evening dress, but without his coat, and brandishing in his hand a recalcitrant white tie.*

Mr Darling (*implying that he has searched for her everywhere and that the nursery is a strange place to find her*) Oh, here you are, Mary.

Mrs Darling (*knowing at once what is the matter*) What is the matter, George, dear?

Mr Darling (*as if the word were monstrous*) Matter! The matter is that I am a desperate man! This tie, it will not tie. (*He waxes sarcastic*) Not round my neck. Round the bed-post, oh yes; twenty times I have made it up round the bed-post, but round my neck oh dear no; begs to be excused.

Michael (*in a joyous transport*) Say it again, Father, say it again!

Mr Darling (*witheringly*) Thank you. (*Goaded by a suspiciously crooked smile on* MRS DARLING's *face*) I warn you, Mary, that unless this tie is round my neck we don't go out to dinner tonight, and if I don't go out to dinner tonight, I never go to the office again, and if I don't go to the office again you and I starve, and our children will be thrown into the streets.

The CHILDREN *blanch as they grasp the gravity of the situation.*

Mrs Darling Let me try, dear.

In a terrible silence their progeny cluster around them. Will she succeed? Their fate depends on it. She fails – no, she succeeds!

Mr Darling Hoop-la!

Everyone Hoop-la!

In another moment they are wildly gay, romping round the room on each other's shoulders. FATHER *is an even better horse than* MOTHER. MICHAEL *is dropped upon his bed,* WENDY *retires to prepare for hers and* JOHN *runs from* NANA, *who has appeared with the bath towel.*

John (*rebellious*) I won't be bathed. You needn't think it.

Mr Darling (*in the grand manner*) Go and be bathed at once, sir.

With bent head JOHN *follows* NANA *into the bathroom.* MR DARLING *swells.*

Michael (*as he is put between the sheets*) Mother, how did you get to know me?

Mr Darling A little less noise there.

Michael (*growing solemn*) At what time was I born, Mother?

Mrs Darling At two o'clock in the night-time, dearest.

Michael Oh, Mother! I hope I didn't wake you.

Mrs Darling They are rather sweet, don't you think, George?

Mr Darling (*doting*) There is not their equal on earth, and they are ours, ours!

Unfortunately NANA *has come in from the bathroom for a sponge and she collides with his trousers, the first pair he has ever had with braid on them.*

Mary, it is too bad; just look at this; covered with hairs. (*Turning on* NANA) Clumsy, clumsy!

NANA *goes, a drooping figure.*

Mrs Darling Let me brush you, dear.

Once more she is successful. They are now by the fire, and MICHAEL *lies quietly in bed, communing with his teddy bear.*

Mr Darling (*depressed*) I sometimes think, Mary, that it is a mistake to have a dog for a nurse.

Mrs Darling (*the opportunity has come for her to tell him of something that is on her mind*) George, we must keep Nana. (*Her seriousness impresses him*) When I came into this room tonight I saw a face at the window.

Mr Darling (*incredulous*) A face at the window, three floors up? Pooh!

Mrs Darling It was the face of a little boy; he was trying to get in.

Mr Darling Impossible! You can't be well, Mary. How many fingers am I holding up?

Mrs Darling Five.

Mr Darling How many now?

Mrs Darling One.

Mr Darling You seem to be all right.

Mrs Darling George, this is not the first time I have seen that boy.

Mr Darling (*beginning to think that this may be a man's job*) Oho!

Mrs Darling The first time was a week ago. It was Nana's night out, and I had been drowsing here by the fire when suddenly I felt a draught, as if the window were open. I looked around and I saw that boy – in the *room*.

Mr Darling In the *room*?

Mrs Darling I screamed. The boy leapt through the window and slammed it behind him. I rushed down into the street to look for his little body on the pavement, but there was nothing there. I thought I must have dreamed it but when I returned to the nursery, there on the floor lay his shadow. He had shut the window so quickly he had cut it clean off.

Mr Darling (*heavily*) Mary, Mary, why didn't you keep that shadow?

Mrs Darling (*scoring*) I did. I rolled it up, George; and here it is.

She produces it from a drawer. They unroll and examine the flimsy thing, which is not more material than a puff of smoke, and if let go would probably float into the ceiling without discolouring it. Yet it has human shape. As they nod their heads over it they present the most satisfying picture on the earth, two happy parents conspiring cosily by the fire for the good of their children.

Mr Darling It is nobody I *know*, but he does look like a scoundrel.

Mrs Darling I think he comes back to get his shadow, George.

Mr Darling (*meaning that the miscreant now has a father to deal with*) There is money in this, my love. I shall take it to the British Museum tomorrow and have it priced.

The shadow is rolled up and replaced in the drawer.

Mrs Darling (*like a guilty person*) George, I have not told you all; I am afraid to.

Mr Darling (*who knows exactly the right moment to treat a woman like a beloved child*) Cowardy, cowardy custard.

Mrs Darling No, I'm not.

Mr Darling Oh yes, you are.

Mrs Darling George, I'm not.

Mr Darling Then why not tell?

Mrs Darling (*thus cleverly soothed she goes on*) The boy was not alone that first time. He was accompanied by – I don't know how to describe it – by a ball of light, no bigger than my fist, but it darted about the room like a living thing.

Mr Darling (*though open-minded*) That is *very* unusual. It escaped with the boy?

Mrs Darling Yes. (*Sliding her hand into his*) George, what can all this mean?

Mr Darling (*ever ready*) What indeed?

This intimate scene is broken by the return of NANA *with a bottle in her mouth.*

Mrs Darling (*at once dissembling*) What is that, Nana? Ah, of course; Michael, it is your medicine.

Michael (*promptly*) Won't take it.

Mr Darling (*recalling his youth*) Be a man, Michael.

Michael Won't.

Mrs Darling (*weakly*) I'll get you a lovely chocky to take after it.

She leaves the room, although her husband calls after her.

Mr Darling Mary, don't pamper him. When I was your age, Michael, I took medicine without a murmur. I said 'Thank you, kind parents, for giving me bottles to make me well.'

WENDY, *who has appeared in her nightgown, hears this and believes.*

Wendy That medicine you sometimes take is much nastier, isn't it, Father?

Mr Darling (*valuing her support*) Ever so much nastier. And as an example to you, Michael, I would take it now ... (*Thankfully*) ... if I hadn't lost the bottle.

Wendy (*always glad to be of service*) I know where it is, Father. I'll fetch it.

She is gone before he can stop her. He turns for help to JOHN, *who has come from the bathroom attired for bed.*

Mr Darling John, it is the most beastly stuff. It is that sticky sweet kind.

John (*who is perhaps still playing at parents*) Never mind, Father, it will soon be over.

A spasm of ill-will to JOHN *cuts through* MR DARLING, *and is gone.* WENDY *returns, panting.*

Wendy Here it is, Father; I have been as quick as I could.

Mr Darling (*with a sarcasm that is completely thrown away on her*) You have been wonderfully quick, precious quick!

He is now at the foot of MICHAEL's *bed.* NANA *is by its side, holding the medicine spoon insinuatingly in her mouth.*

Wendy (*proudly, as she pours out* MR DARLING's *medicine*) Michael, now you will see how father takes it.

Mr Darling (*hedging*) Michael first.

Michael (*full of unworthy suspicions*) Father first.

Mr Darling It will make me sick, you know.

John (*lightly*) Come on, Father.

Mr Darling Hold your tongue, sir.

Wendy (*disturbed*) I thought you took it quite easily, Father, saying 'Thank you, kind parents, for giving me bot...'

Mr Darling (*interrupting*) That is not the point! The point is that there is more in my glass than in Michael's spoon. It isn't fair! I *swear* though it were with my last breath, it is not fair.

Michael (*coldly*) Father, I'm waiting.

Mr Darling It's all very well to say you are waiting; so am I waiting.

Michael Father's a cowardy custard.

Mr Darling So you are a cowardy custard.

They are now glaring at each other.

Michael I am not frightened.

Mr Darling Neither am *I* frightened.

Michael Well, then, *take* it.

Mr Darling Well, then, *you* take it.

Wendy (*butting in again*) Why not take it at the same time?

Mr Darling (*haughtily*) Certainly. Are you ready, Michael?

Wendy (*as nothing has happened*) One – two – three.

MICHAEL *partakes, but* MR DARLING *resorts to hanky-panky.*

John Father hasn't taken his!

MICHAEL *howls and stamps off to his bed in high dudgeon.*

Wendy (*inexpressibly pained*) Oh, Father!

Mr Darling (*who has been hiding the glass behind him*) What do you mean by 'Oh, Father'? I meant to take it but I missed it. Michael, stop that row!

NANA *shakes her head sadly over him, and goes into the bathroom. They are all looking as if they did not admire him, and nothing so dashes a temperamental man.*

Mr Darling I say, I have just thought of a splendid joke.

They brighten.

I shall pour my medicine into Nana's bowl and she will drink it thinking it is milk!

The pleasantry does not appeal, but he prepares the joke, undismayed.

Michael (*howling again*) Father!

Wendy Poor darling Nana!

John (*at the same time*) Bad form, Father.

Mr Darling You silly little things; I am ashamed of you.

They steal to their beds as MRS DARLING *returns with the chocolate, followed by* LIZA, *who proceeds to collect the hot-water bottles from the children's beds.*

Mrs Darling Well, is it all over?

Michael Father didn't –

MR DARLING *glares.*

Mr Darling All over, dear, quite satisfactorily.

NANA *comes back.*

Mr Darling (*bursting with amusement*) Nana, good dog, good girl; I have put a little milk into your bowl.

MR DARLING *has put the bowl right in the middle of the carpet where the joke will be unmissable.* NANA *bounds over to the bowl and begins to lap, but only begins. She splutters and coughs and retreats into the kennel.*

Mrs Darling What is the matter, Nana?

Mr Darling (*uneasily*) Nothing, nothing.

Mrs Darling (*smelling the bowl*) George, it is your medicine!

The CHILDREN *break into lamentation.* MR DARLING *gives his wife an imploring look; he is begging for one smile, but does not get it. In consequence he goes from bad to worse.*

Mr Darling It was only a joke. Much good my wearing myself to the bone trying to be funny in this house.

Wendy (*on her knees by the kennel*) Father, Nana is crying.

Mr Darling Coddle her; nobody coddles me. Oh dear no. I am only the breadwinner, why should I be coddled? Why, why, why?

Mrs Darling George, not so loud; the servants will hear you.

LIZA *leaves the room with an armful of hot-water bottles, and a distinct sniff in the direction of* MR DARLING.

Mr Darling (*defiant*) Let them hear me; bring in the whole world.

The desperate man, who has not been in fresh air for days, has now lost all self-control.

I refuse to allow that dog to lord it in my nursery for one hour longer.

NANA *supplicates him.*

Mr Darling In vain, in vain, the proper place for you is the yard, and there you go to be tied up this instant.

NANA *again retreats into the kennel, and the children add their prayers to hers.*

Mrs Darling (*who knows how contrite he will be for this presently*) George, remember what I told you about that boy.

Mr Darling Am I master in this house or is she? (*To* NANA *fiercely*) Come along.

He thunders at her, but she indicates that she has reasons not worth troubling him with for remaining where she is. He resorts to a false bonhomie.

There, there, did she think he was angry with her, poor Nana?

She wriggles a response in the affirmative.

Good Nana, pretty Nana.

She has seldom been called pretty, and it has the old effect. She plays rub-a-dub with her paws, which is how a dog blushes.

She will come to her kind master, won't she? Won't she?

She advances, retreats, waggles her head, her tail, and eventually goes to him. He seizes her collar in an iron grip and amid the cries of his progeny drags her from the room.

Mr Darling Come along!

Children Father!

They listen, for NANA's *remonstrances are not inaudible.*

Mrs Darling Be brave, my dears.

Wendy He is chaining Nana up!

This unfortunately is what he is doing, though we cannot see him. Let us hope that he then retires to his study, looks up the word 'temper' in his thesaurus, and under the influence of those benign pages becomes a better man. In the meantime the children have been put to bed in unwonted silence and MRS DARLING *tucks them in.*

John (*as the barking below goes on*) She is awfully unhappy.

Wendy That is not Nana's unhappy bark. That is her bark when she smells danger.

Mrs Darling (*remembering that boy*) Danger! Are you sure, Wendy?

Wendy (*the one of the family, for there is one in every family, who can be trusted to know or not to know*) Oh yes.

Mrs Darling (*half to herself*) Oh, how I wish I was not going out to dinner tonight.

Michael Can anything harm us, Mother, after the night-lights are lit?

Mrs Darling Nothing, precious. They are the eyes a mother leaves behind her to guard her children.

Nevertheless we may be sure she means to tell LIZA *to look in on them frequently till she comes home. She goes from bed to bed, after her custom, lighting the night-lights and crooning a lullaby.*

> In the quiet of the night
> May the wanderers see a light
> That will lead them safely on
> To the shelter of their home . . .

Michael (*drowsily*) Mother, I'm glad of you.

Mrs Darling:
> And with all their perils past
> May they reach their home at last.

(*With a last look round, her hand on the switch*) Dear night-lights that protect my sleeping babes, burn clear and steadfast tonight.

The nursery darkens and she is gone, intentionally leaving the door ajar. Something uncanny is going to happen, we expect, for a quiver has passed through the room, just sufficient to touch the night-lights. They blink three times one after the other and go out, precisely as the children (whom familiarity has made them resemble) fall asleep. Then from far away in the night sky comes another light, at first no bigger than one of the larger stars. As it draws closer, it seems to bring a gust of wind with it, for the nursery window starts to rattle, and the light flits into the room. It is no larger than Mrs Darling's fist and in the time we have taken to say this, it has been into the drawers and wardrobe and searched pockets, as it darts about looking for a certain shadow. Then, quite suddenly, the window is blown open, probably by the smallest and therefore most mischievous star, and PETER PAN *flies into the room. In so far as he is dressed at all, it is in autumn leaves and cobwebs. As* PETER *lands on the nursery floor,* JOHN *moves in his sleep. Startled,* PETER *slips into the bathroom, and watches* JOHN *carefully through the half-closed door.* JOHN *doesn't wake up, so* PETER *comes back into the room. (A subtle adjustment has been made to his costume, but we don't notice it at all.)*

Peter *(in a whisper)* Tinker Bell, Tink, where are you?

A jug lights up and TINKER BELL's *answer comes from it as a tinkle of bells. This is the fairy language.* PETER *can speak it, but it bores him. We can just make out* TINKER BELL's *words, but never clearly enough to be quite sure of what she is saying, which is just as well, perhaps, as her expressions are sometimes not altogether refined.*

Tinker Bell I'm in here.

Peter Oh, do come out of that jug.

TINKER BELL *flashes hither and thither.*

Peter Do you know where they put it?

Tinker Bell In the big box.

Peter Which big box?

Tinker Bell (*hovering over the chest of drawers*) Over here.

Peter This one?

Tinker Bell Yes.

Peter But which drawer?

Tinker Bell (*teasing*) I'll show you if you like.

Peter Yes, do show me.

TINKER BELL *pulls at one of the drawers; the one* MR DARLING *put the shadow in. After a couple of tugs it pulls open and* PETER *starts rummaging through it, scattering its contents to the floor, as kings on their wedding day toss ha'pence to the crowd.* TINKER BELL *hops into the drawer and joins in the search.*

Tinker Bell It's just in here, under these things, they've tucked it away – it's here somewhere – (*She sneezes*) Ugh ... dusty – and that awful smell of lavend- ...

PETER *pulls out the shadow and turns joyfully away from the chest of drawers, slamming the drawer shut as he goes.* TINKER BELL, *unfortunately, is still inside it.*

Tinker Bell (*her voice suddenly smothered*) ... Oof!

PETER *lays the shadow out on the floor and stands on its feet, confident that he and it will join like drops of water. He walks across the floor but the shadow, alas, will not follow. He repeats the operation, this time with a fierce concentration of mind and foot. The shadow remains, as lifeless as ever. Then he darts into the bathroom, returning at once with a bar of soap and a long-handled scrubbing brush. He applies soap to the soles of his feet with the brush and tries to stick the shadow to them but this method fails him too. A shudder passes through him and he subsides dejectedly to the floor and starts to cry. This wakens WENDY, who sits up, and is pleasantly interested to see a stranger.*

Wendy (*courteously*) Boy, why are you crying?

PETER *jumps up, and crossing to the foot of the bed bows to her in the fairy way. WENDY, impressed, bows to him from the bed.*

Peter What is your name?

Wendy (*well-satisfied*) Wendy Moira Angela Darling. What is yours?

Peter (*finding it lamentably brief*) Peter Pan.

Wendy Is that all?

Peter (*biting his lip*) Yes.

Wendy (*politely*) I am so sorry.

Peter It doesn't matter.

Wendy Where do you live?

Peter Second on the right and straight on till morning.

Wendy What a funny address!

Peter No, it isn't.

Wendy (*not wanting to offend*) I mean, is that what they put on the letters?

Peter Don't get any letters.

Wendy But your mother gets letters?

Peter Don't have a mother.

Wendy (*appalled*) Peter!

She leaps out of bed to put her arms round him, but he draws back.

No wonder you were crying.

Peter I wasn't crying about my mother. I was crying because I can't get my shadow to stick on. Anyway I wasn't crying.

Wendy It has come off! How awful.

Looking at the spot where the vain operation has taken place, WENDY *laughs gleefully.*

Peter, you have been trying to stick it on with soap!

Peter (*snappily*) Well, then?

Wendy It must be sewn on.

Peter What is 'sewn'?

Wendy You are dreadfully ignorant.

Peter No, I'm not.

Wendy I will sew it on for you, my little man.

She goes to her bedside cabinet and retrieves a neatly ordered sewing basket from which she selects a needle and thread.

PETER *blenches at the sight of the needle, and starts to draw away.*

Wendy Stand still. I dare say it will hurt a little.

Peter (*a recent remark of hers rankling*) I never cry.

WENDY *sews the shadow to his heels,* PETER *clenching his teeth against the pain.*

Wendy There!

PETER *walks about the nursery, but the flimsy thing drags uselessly behind him.*

Peter It isn't quite itself yet.

Wendy Perhaps I should have ironed it.

Peter Perhaps it's dead.

Wendy I think we need a little more light.

She touches something and to his astonishment the room is illuminated. The shadow awakens and is glad to be back with him as he is to have it. PETER *and his shadow dance together. He is showing off now. He crows like a cock. He would fly in order to impress* WENDY *further if he knew that there is anything unusual in that.*

Peter Wendy, look, look; oh the cleverness of me!

Wendy You conceit; of course I did nothing!

Peter You did a little.

Wendy (*wounded*) A little! If I am no use I can at least withdraw.

With one haughty leap she is again in bed with the sheet over her face. Popping on to the end of the bed the artful one appeals.

Peter Wendy, don't withdraw. I can't help crowing, Wendy, when I'm pleased with myself. (*A sudden inspiration*) Wendy, one girl is worth more than twenty boys.

Wendy (*peeping over the sheet*) You really think so, Peter?

Peter Yes, I do.

Wendy I think it's perfectly sweet of you, and I shall get up again.

They sit together on the side of the bed.

I shall give you a kiss if you like.

Peter Thank you.

He holds out his hand.

Wendy (*aghast*) Don't you know what a kiss is?

Peter I shall know when you give it to me.

Not to hurt his feelings, she gives him her thimble.

Now shall I give you a kiss?

Wendy (*primly*) If you please.

He pulls an acorn button off his person and bestows it on her. She is shocked but considerate.

I will wear it on this chain around my neck. Peter, how old are you?

Peter (*blithely*) I don't know, but quite young, Wendy. I ran away the day I was born.

Wendy Ran away, why?

Peter Because I heard father and mother talking of what I was to be when I became a man. Wendy, I want always to be a little boy and to have fun; so I ran away to Kensington Gardens and lived a long time among the fairies.

Wendy (*with great eyes*) You know fairies, Peter!

Peter (*surprised that this should be a recommendation*) Yes, but they are nearly all dead now. (*Baldly*) You see, Wendy, when the first baby laughed for the first time, the laugh broke into a thousand pieces, and they all went skipping about, and that was the beginning of fairies. And now when every new baby is born its first laugh becomes a fairy. So there ought to be a fairy for every boy or girl.

Wendy (*breathlessly*) Ought to be? Isn't there?

Peter Oh no. Children know such a lot now. Soon they don't believe in fairies, and every time a child says 'I don't believe in fairies' there is a fairy somewhere that falls down dead. (*Heartlessly*) They just crumple up.

Wendy Poor things!

Peter (*to whom this statement recalls a forgotten friend*) I can't think where she has gone. Tinker Bell! Tink! Where are you?

TINKER BELL *answers from the drawer but her words are, luckily, inaudible.*

Wendy (*thrilling*) Peter, you don't mean to tell me that there is a fairy in this room!

Peter (*with shameless glee*) Wendy, I believe I shut her up in that drawer!

He releases TINKER BELL, *who darts about the room in a fury, using language not at all flattering to* PETER.

Peter You needn't say that; I'm very sorry, but how could I know you were in the drawer?

Wendy (*her eyes dancing in pursuit of the delicious creature*) Oh, Peter, if only she would stand still and let me see her.

Peter (*indifferently*) They hardly ever stand still.

Tinker Bell (*just to prove that she can*) Oh, yes we do.

Wendy I see her, the lovely!

WENDY *approaches, putting out a hand to touch, but* TINK *darts away from her with dizzying speed, so close to her face that she can feel the breeze of* TINK's *wings.*

Wendy Oooh! (*Looking round the room*) Where is she now?

Peter Behind the clock. (*Insinuatingly, making the elementary mistake of trying to please both females at the same time*) Tink ... this lady wishes you were her fairy.

The answer comes immediately.

Wendy What does she say?

Peter She is not very polite. She says you are a great ugly girl, and that she is my fairy. You know, Tink, you can't be my fairy because I am a gentleman and you are a lady.

Tinker Bell You silly ass!

Wendy What did she say?

Peter She said 'You silly ass.' She is quite a common girl, you know.

Tinker Bell Ah!

Peter She is called Tinker Bell because she mends the fairy pots and kettles.

Tinker Bell Common! How dare you? You nasty, spiteful little boy – how dare you say so? Common!

She storms off down the picture rail and drops back into the jug, a comfortable place for a sulk. WENDY *decides that the best policy will be to ignore* TINK *for the time being.*

Wendy Where do you live now?

Peter With the lost boys.

Wendy Who are they?

Peter They are the children who fall out of their prams when their nanny is looking the other way. If they are not claimed in seven days they are sent away to the Never Land. I'm captain.

Wendy What fun it must be.

Peter (*craftily*) Yes, but we are rather lonely. You see, Wendy, we have no female companionship.

Wendy Are none of the other children girls?

Peter Oh no; girls, you know, are much too clever to fall out of their prams.

Wendy Peter, it is perfectly lovely the way you talk about girls. John there just despises us.

PETER, *for the first time, has a good look at* JOHN. *He then crosses the room and neatly tumbles him out of the bed.*

Wendy You wicked! You are not captain here.

She bends over her brother who is prone on the floor.

After all, he hasn't wakened, and you meant to be kind.

Having done her duty she forgets JOHN, *who blissfully sleeps on.*

Peter, you may give me a kiss.

Peter (*cynically*) I thought you would want it back.

He offers her the thimble.

Wendy (*artfully*) Oh dear, I didn't mean a kiss, Peter, I meant a thimble.

Peter (*only half placated*) What is that?

Wendy It is like this.

She kisses him.

Peter (*satisfied*) Now shall I give you a thimble?

Wendy If you please.

Before he can even draw near she screams.

Aagh!

Peter What is it?

Wendy It was exactly as if someone were pulling my hair.

And indeed it is, for TINK *has done just that, flitting across the room almost too quickly for us to see.*

Peter That must have been Tink. I never knew her so naughty before.

Tinker Bell (*back on the picture rail again*) And I'll pull it again, *harder*, every time she gives you a thimble. Ugh! Disgusting!

Wendy What does she say?

Peter She says she will do that every time I give you a thimble.

Wendy But why?

Peter (*equally nonplussed*) Why, Tink?

Tinker Bell (*almost derisive*) You silly ass!

Peter She said 'You silly ass' again.

Wendy (*beginning to understand the strength of her rival*) She is very impertinent.

TINK *laughs and hops back into the jug.* PETER *and* WENDY *are now sitting on the floor.*

Wendy Peter, why did you come to *our* nursery window?

Peter To try to hear stories. None of us knows any stories.

Wendy How perfectly awful!

Peter That's why swallows build in the eaves of houses – to listen to the stories. Wendy, your mother was telling you such a lovely story.

Wendy Which story was it?

Peter About the prince, and he couldn't find the lady who wore the glass slipper.

Wendy That was *Cinderella*. Peter, he found her and they were happy ever after.

Peter I am glad.

They have worked their way along the floor close to each

other, but now he jumps up.

Wendy Peter, where are you going?

Peter (*already on his way to the window*) To tell the other boys.

Wendy Don't go, Peter. I know lots of stories. The stories I could tell to the boys!

Peter (*gleaming*) Come with me then. We'll fly.

Wendy Fly? You can fly!

How he would like to rip those stories out of her; he is dangerous now.

Peter Yes.

Wendy Oh dear, I mustn't. Think of mother.

Peter You shall! You shall!

He seizes her.

Wendy Let go, Peter Pan. Besides, I can't fly.

Peter I'll teach you.

Wendy But I won't go away with you.

Peter You won't be able to help it!

Wendy Then I won't *learn*.

She pulls away from him and retreats to the bed with dignity, tidily tucking herself away from the dangerous boy.

Peter I'll teach you how to jump on the wind's back, and then away we go – and if there are more winds than one they toss you about in the sky – they fling you miles and miles – but you always fall soft on to another wind – and sometimes you go crashing through the tops of trees, scaring the owls – and if you meet a boy's kite in the air you shove your foot through it. The stars are giving a party tonight! (*Turning on her with an amazed disdain*) Oh, Wendy, when you are sleeping in your silly bed you might be flying about with me playing hide and seek with the stars! (*Trying a new tack*) And, Wendy, there are mermaids.

Wendy (*taking the bait*) Mermaids, with tails?

Peter Such long tails.

Wendy Oh, to see a mermaid.

She just succeeds in remaining inside the covers.

Peter Wendy, you could tuck us in at night.

Wendy (*slowly emerging from the bed*) Oo!

Peter None of us has ever been tucked in at night.

Wendy (*and a little bit more*) Oo!

Peter And make pockets for us. None of us has any pockets. Wendy, how we should all respect you.

At this she strikes her colours, joining PETER *on the nursery floor.*

Wendy Of course, it's awfully fascinating! Would you teach John and Michael to fly too?

Peter (*indifferently*) If you like.

Wendy I don't promise to go away with you. I don't think there's the least chance of my going.

Peter (*craftily*) All right.

Wendy (*playing rum-tum on* JOHN) John, wake up. There is a boy here who is to teach us to fly.

John Is there? Then I shall get up.

He raises his head from the floor.

Hullo, I am up.

Wendy Michael, open your eyes.

She prises MICHAEL'*s eyes open.*

This boy is to teach us to fly.

The sleepers are at once as awake as their father's razor; but before a question can be asked NANA'*s bark is heard.*

Michael Nana!

John (*to* PETER) Quick, hide! Out with the light!

Wendy (*whispering to* JOHN) Pillows in beds!

Peter (*repeating everything he hears, because of the fun of it*) Out with the light! Quick! Pillows in beds! Hide!

Wendy Shhh!

Peter Shhh!

The bedclothes and pillows are arranged to deceive...

John Into the bathroom!

Peter Into the bathroom! Shhh!

... and then the four deceivers run across the nursery and hide in the bathroom. When LIZA *enters with a firm hand on the troubled* NANA'*s chain, the room is in comparative darkness.*

Liza There, you suspicious brute, they are perfectly safe, aren't they? Every one of the little angels sound asleep in bed. Listen to their gentle breathing.

NANA's *sense of smell here helps to her undoing instead of hindering it. She knows that they are in the bathroom, and breaks from her keeper's control, hurling herself against the bathroom door.*

Liza No more of it, Nana. (*She pulls* NANA *away from the door and wags a stern finger at her*) I warn you, if you bark again I shall go straight for master and missus and bring them home from the party, and then won't the master whip you just! Come along, you naughty dog!

The unhappy NANA *is hauled away. The* CHILDREN *emerge exultant from the bathroom. In their brief absence from the scene strange things have been done to them; but it is not for us to reveal a mysterious secret of the stage. They look just the same.*

John (*ever the doubtful one*) I say, can you *really* fly?

Peter Look!

He is now over their heads.

John How splendid!

Wendy Oh, how sweet!

Peter I'm sweet! Oh, I am sweet!

It looks so easy that they try it first from the floor and then from their beds, without encouraging results.

John (*rubbing his knees*) How do you do it?

Peter (*descending*) You just think lovely wonderful thoughts and they lift you up in the air. Look.

He is off again.

John You are so nippy at it; couldn't you do it very slowly once?

PETER *obliges, landing a few inches from* JOHN's *nose.*

John I've got it now, Wendy.

He tries; no, he has not got it, poor stay-at-home, though he knows the names of all the counties in England and Peter does not know one.

Peter I must blow the fairy dust on you first. Where are you, Tink?

TINK *is on the mantelpiece, surveying the flying lessons with the natural disdain of an expert.* PETER *grabs her and teases some of her fairy dust on to his hand.*

Tinker Bell (*giggling*) Peter, stop it! Get off!

Music, as PETER *blows dust on each of the* CHILDREN, *who shiver with delight as the sparkly stuff settles on them.*

Peter Now, try; try from the bed. Just wriggle your shoulders this way, and then let go.

The gallant MICHAEL *is the first to let go, and is borne across the room.*

Michael (*with a yell that should have disturbed* LIZA) I flewed!

JOHN *lets go, and swims across the room with a fine breaststroke. He meets* WENDY *coming the other way though they had both aimed in an opposite direction.*

John (*tending to be upside down*) How ripping!

Wendy Eeeeeh! Lovely!

Michael (*playing whack on a bed*) I do like it!

The Three Look at me! Look at me! Look at me!

They are not nearly as elegant in the air as PETER, *but their heads have bumped the ceiling, and there is nothing more delicious than that.*

John (*landing by his bed*) I say, why shouldn't we go out?

Peter There are pirates.

John Pirates! (*He grabs his tall Sunday hat*) Let us go at once!

Peter (*as if he had heard the little star whisper 'cave'*) Altogether then!

From down below in the street the lighted window must present an unwonted spectacle; the shadows of CHILDREN *revolving in the room like a merry-go-round. This is perhaps what* MR *and* MRS DARLING *see as they come hurrying home from the party, brought by* NANA *who, you may be sure, has broken her chain. Peter's accomplice, the little star, has seen them coming, and again the window blows open.*

PETER *breaks from the circle first and flies out of the window, over the trees of the square and up over the house-tops, the others following like a flight of birds.*

Peter Second to the right, and straight on till morning!

The broken-hearted MRS DARLING *arrives just in time to get a nip from* TINK *as she too sets out for the Never Land. The nursery disappears from view and the four* CHILDREN *are left flying through the night sky. The Houses of Parliament underneath them. They circle round the tower of Big Ben, just to say they have done it, and fly up into the clouds.*

John Come on, Michael, let's race. I'll give you a start.

MICHAEL *sets off at a terrific pace, swiftly followed by* JOHN.

Michael (*suddenly stopping*) Ow! Wendy!

Wendy What is it?

Michael My head hurts.

Peter (*diving past them*) Well, stop bumping into the clouds, silly!

John (*to* WENDY) I say, what a swank!

Wendy Do be more polite to him.

John Then tell him to stop showing off.

Half asleep, MICHAEL *begins to plummet earthwards.*

Wendy Michael!

John He's fallen asleep!

Wendy Peter! Save him!

PETER *swoops down and returns with a dazed* MICHAEL.

Wendy Oh, Peter, you're wonderful!

Peter Yes I am! What's your name?

Wendy I'm Wendy!

Peter I say, Wendy, if you see me forgetting you, just keep on saying 'I'm Wendy' and then I'll remember.

PETER *soars away from them. The three* CHILDREN *are*

left behind, holding hands for comfort, and beginning to feel rather small.

John What a cheek!

Wendy You must be nice to him. What could we do if he were to leave us?

Michael (*a little hopefully*) We could go back.

Wendy How could we ever find our way back without him?

John Well, then, we could go on.

Wendy That is the awful thing, John. We should have to go on, for we don't know how to stop!

The STORYTELLER *appears in the darkness beneath them.*

Storyteller So on, and on, and on they flew, over their second sea and through their third night, Peter teaching them how to sleep on the wind, and say fearfully funny things to the stars. And after many moons they drew near to the Never Land at last.

Peter There it is!

The Three What? Where? Where?

Peter The Never Land! Stand on tiptoe and you'll see it.

They all stand on tiptoe in the air.

Wendy John! There's a lagoon!

John Turtles, Wendy, burying their eggs in the sand!

Michael I say, John, I see a flamingo with a broken leg!

John Look, Michael, a cave!

Wendy John, what's that in the brushwood?

John (*always knowledgeable*) It's a wolf with her whelps!

Michael I say, John, is that the smoke of a redskin camp?

John Where? Show me! Are they on the warpath?

Wendy There! Just across the mysterious river.

John I see now. Yes, they're on the warpath right enough!

Wendy Michael, what's *that*?

Michael It's a pirate ship!

The air is suddenly rent by the most tremendous crash they have ever heard. The roar of it echoes through the mountains and the echoes seem to cry savagely, 'Where are they, where are they, where are they?' Thus sharply do the terrified CHILDREN learn the difference between an island of make-believe, and the same island come true. They are buffeted around in the air as the cannonballs hurtle past them. PETER merely dodges these familiar missiles, treating them as so many playmates. At last the heavens are steady again.

Peter Pirates!

John (*to* MICHAEL) Are you shot?

Michael I haven't tried yet.

Peter If you like we'll go down and kill one.

John (*instantly excited*) I say, do you kill many?

Peter Tons!

John How ripping! Are there a lot of them?

Peter I've never known so many!

John (*a niggling doubt*) Who is captain now?

Peter Hook.

John (*quailing at the name*) James Hook?

Peter Aye.

John (*huskily*) He was Blackbeard's bo'sun.

Peter Well, do you want an adventure now, or would you like to have your tea first?

The Three (*after a slight pause for thought*) Tea first!

PETER *and the* CHILDREN *fly up and away.*

ACT TWO
The Never Land

Enter the STORYTELLER. *Behind him is the Never Land, shrouded in darkness. Music. When the scene starts all is so dark that you scarcely know it has begun. Then Peter's star wakes up, and in the blink of it, which is much stronger than in our stars, you can begin to make out the Never Land. You have often half seen it before, or even three-quarters, after the night-lights were lit, and you might then have beached your coracle on it if you had not always at the great moment fallen asleep.*

Storyteller What you can just make out through the clouds is the Never Land. If you were to see it – bang – the wonders of it might hurt your eyes.

If you all came in spectacles perhaps you could see it bang, but to make a rule of that kind would be a pity.

You can just make out masses of trees and you think you see wild beasts stealing past to drink, and mermaids basking in the lagoon beyond the trees, carefully combing their hair; not really far away, for the Never Land is very compact, not large and sprawly with tedious distances between one adventure and another, but nicely crammed.

It is winter time on the river and summer on the lagoon.

This is not remarkable on Peter's island where all the four seasons may pass while you are filling a jug at the well.

In the daytime you think the Never Land is only make-believe, and so it is to the likes of you, but *this* is the Never Land come true.

The island comes into full view, and the STORYTELLER *walks about upon it.*

The beasts were out looking for the redskins, the redskins were looking for the pirates, the pirates were looking for the lost boys and they were all going round and round the island.

And so do we go round and round the island, until we have seen all of it, and the STORYTELLER *is quite worn out with the unaccustomed exercise.*

Peter's home is at this very spot, but can you point out the way into it? Even if I told you which is the entrance? Even if I told you there were seven entrances? The holes in these seven tree-stumps are the 'doors' down to Peter's home under the ground! He made seven because he thought seven boys must need seven doors!

One of the lost boys, SLIGHTLY, *emerges from his tree-stump, perhaps driven from the abode below by companions less musical than himself.*

The biggest door belongs to the biggest boy, who is called Slightly and is quite possibly a genius. He cuts whistles out of the trees and then dances to his own tunes.

SLIGHTLY *plays his whistle, to which he capers entrancingly, with no audience save a* NEVER OSTRICH *which is also musically inclined. Unable to imitate* SLIGHTLY's *graces, the bird falls so low as to burlesque them and is driven from the entertainment.* TOOTLES *appears from his hole.*

Storyteller Tootles is not the least brave, though the most unfortunate of the gallant band. He has been in fewer adventures than the others because the big things constantly happen while he has stepped around the corner. He will go off in some quiet hour to gather firewood and when he returns the others will be sweeping up the blood.

Instead of souring his nature this has sweetened it and he is the humblest of the band.

Tootles Has Peter come back yet, Slightly?

Slightly (*with a solemnity that he thinks suits the occasion*) No, Tootles, no.

Nibs *appears...*

Storyteller Next is Nibs, the gay and debonair.

... and so does CURLY.

Curly is a pickle, and so often has he had to deliver up his person when Peter said 'Stand forth the one who did this thing!', that he now stands forth whether he has done it or not. The other two are First Twin...

FIRST TWIN *pops up out of his tree-stump ...*

Storyteller ...and Second Twin...

... and pops back in again while SECOND TWIN *pops out.*

... who cannot be described because we should probably be describing the wrong one.

Finally FIRST TWIN *pops out next to* SECOND TWIN, *giving both of them a fright.*

Storyteller There were six of them altogether, counting the twins as two, and tonight they were awaiting their Captain's return.

They are all dressed in the skins of animals they think they have shot, and so round and furry in them that if they fall they roll. Hunkering on the ground or peeping out of their holes, the six are not unlike village gossips gathered round the pump or like dogs waiting for the master to tell them that the day has begun.

Curly (*as if* PETER *might be listening*) I do wish Peter would come back.

Tootles I am always afraid of the pirates when Peter is not here to protect us.

Slightly I am not afraid of pirates. Nothing frightens me. But I do wish Peter would come back and tell us whether he has heard anything more about Cinderella.

Second Twin (*with diffidence*) Slightly, I dreamt last night that the Prince found Cinderella.

First Twin (*who is intellectually the superior of the two*) Twin, I think you should not have dreamt that, for I didn't, and Peter may say . . .

Both Twins . . . we ought not to dream differently, being twins . . .

First Twin . . . you know?

Tootles I am awfully anxious about Cinderella. You see, not knowing anything about my mother I am fond of thinking that she was rather like Cinderella.

This is received with derision.

Nibs (*the well-born*) All I remember about my mother is that she often said to father, 'Oh, how I wish I had a cheque book of my own.' I don't know what a cheque book is, but I should just love to give my mother one.

Slightly (*who is conceited, and thinks he remembers the days before he was lost with their manners and customs*) My mother was fonder of me than your mothers were of you.

Uproar.

Oh yes, she was. Peter had to make up names for you, but my mother had wrote my name on my pinafore I was lost in. 'Slightly Soiled'; that's my name.

They fall upon him pugnaciously; not because they are really worried about their mothers, who are now as important to them as a piece of string, but because any excuse is good enough for a shindy. Not for long is he belaboured, for a nearby sound is heard that sends them scurrying for their holes.

Pirates
Yo ho, yo ho, the pirate life
The flag of skull and bones
A merry hour, a hempen rope –

Tootles Pirates!

Pirates
And hey for Davy Jones!

In a second of time the scene is bereft of human life. The only boy not to gain the safety of the underground home is NIBS, *who is cut off from his tree-stump by the arrival of the first pirates.*

Storyteller What the lost boys have heard is a verse of the dreadful song with which the pirates stealthily trumpet their approach! A more villainous looking brotherhood of man never hung in a row on Execution Dock!

The PIRATES *come forward, one at a time, combing the landscape for any sign of the children, and proudly colluding with the* STORYTELLER's *description of them.*

In advance of the rest is the handsome Italian Cecco . . .

His great arms are bare, pieces of eight in his ears as ornaments.

Cecco . . . who cut his name in letters of blood in the back of the governor of the prison at Goa.

Storyteller Here is Bill Jukes, every inch of him tattooed . . .

Jukes (*relishing the memory*) . . . the same Jukes who got sixty lashes on the Walrus from Flint before he would drop the bag of gold moidores.

Storyteller Cookson, said to be Black Murphy's brother . . .

Cookson (*twitching with nervousness*) . . . but this was never proved!

Storyteller And Gentleman Starkey, once an usher at a public school . . .

Starkey . . . and still dainty in his ways of killing.

Storyteller Robert Mullins, famous for playing skittles with the mate of the Switch . . .

Robert Mullins . . . for each other's heads!

Storyteller Chay Turley, who laughed with the wrong side of his mouth . . .

Chay Turley (*absurdly vainglorious*) . . . having no other!

Storyteller And Noodler, whose hands were ... er ...

Noodler ... fixed on backwards!

Storyteller And lastly, the boatswain Smee, an oddly genial man, who stabbed, so to speak, without offence ...

Smee (*oddly genial*) ... and the only non-conformist in Hook's whole crew!

Storyteller But the cruellest jewel in this dark setting is Captain James Hook himself.

Stately music, as HOOK is borne forward on his great and sinister chair by four of his strongest men. He is gently lowered to the ground and sits in deepest solitude. Cadaverous and blackavised, he has an iron hook instead of a right hand, and it is with this he claws. The elegance of his diction and the distinction of his demeanour, show him as one of a different class from his crew, a solitary among uncultured companions. A man of indomitable courage, the only thing at which he flinches is the sight of his own blood, which is thick and of an unusual colour. At his public school they said of him that he 'bled yellow'. In dress he apes the dandiacal associated with Charles II, having heard it said in an earlier period of his career that he bore a strange resemblance to the ill-fated Stuarts.

Storyteller Educated at Eton and Oxford – and later a Member of Parliament – the traditions of his class still cling to him. He's never more sinister than when he's most polite. Even his victims on the high seas note that he always says 'sorry' when prodding them along the plank. Above all he retains a passion for good form. 'Good form!' He knows that this is all that really matters.

NIBS is seen for a moment near the lagoon, and STARKEY's

pistol is at once upraised. CAPTAIN HOOK *twists the hook in him.*

Starkey (*abject*) Captain, let go!

Hook Put down that pistol first!

Starkey 'Twas one of those boys you hate; I could have shot him dead.

Hook Ay, and the sound would have brought Tiger Lily's redskins on us. Do you want to lose your scalp?

A murmur of uneasy assent runs through the pirate band.

Smee (*wriggling his cutlass pleasantly*) That is true. Shall I after him, Captain, and tickle him with Johnny Corkscrew? Johnny is a silent fellow.

Hook Bad form, Smee. Besides, he is only one, and I want to mischief all the seven. Scatter and look for them.

The boatswain whistles his instructions and the men disperse on their frightful errand, continuing in their distasteful song.

Pirates
> Avast, belay, yo ho, heave to
> A-pirating we go
> And if we're parted by a shot
> We're sure to meet below!

With none to hear save SMEE, HOOK *becomes confidential.*

Hook Most of all, I want their captain, Peter Pan. 'Twas he cut off my arm. I have waited long to shake his hand with this. (*Luxuriating*) Oh, I'll tear him!

Smee (*always ready for a chat*) Yet I have oft heard you say your hook was worth a score of hands, for combing the hair and other homely uses.

Hook If I was a mother I would pray to have my children born with *this* instead of *that*.

His left arm creeps nervously behind him. He has a galling remembrance.

Smee, Pan flung my arm to a crocodile that happened to be passing by.

Smee I have often noticed your strange dread of crocodiles.

Hook (*pettishly*) Not of crocodiles but of that one crocodile.

He lays bare a lacerated heart.

The brute liked my arm so much, Smee, that he has followed me ever since, from sea to sea, and from land to land, licking his lips for the rest of me.

Smee (*looking for the bright side*) In a way it is a sort of a compliment.

Hook (*with dignity*) I want no such compliments; I want Peter Pan, who first gave the brute his taste for me. Smee, that Crocodile would have had me before now, but by a lucky chance he swallowed a clock, and it goes tick, tick, tick, tick inside him; and so before he can reach me I hear the tick and bolt. (*He emits a hollow rumble*) Once I heard it strike six within him.

Smee (*sombrely*) Some day the clock will run down, and then he'll get you.

hook (*a broken man*) Ay, that is the fear that haunts me. (*He* *rises*) Smee, this seat is hot; odds, bobs, hammer and tongs, I am burning.

He has been sitting, he thinks, on one of the island mush-rooms, which are of enormous size. But this is a hand-painted one placed here in times of danger to conceal a chimney. They remove it, and tell-tale smoke issues; also, alas, the sound of children's voices.

Smee A chimney!

Hook (*avidly*) Listen! Smee, 'tis plain they live here, beneath the ground. There can be but one room below, for there is but one chimney. The silly moles had not the sense to see that they did not need a door apiece. This proves they have no mother!

SMEE *replaces the mushroom,* HOOK *torturously working his brain.*

Smee (*hopefully*) Unrip your plan, Captain.

Hook To return to the boat and cook a large rich cake of jolly thickness with sugar on it, green sugar. We must leave the cake on the shore of the mermaids' lagoon. These boys are always swimming about there, trying to catch the mermaids. They will find the cake and gobble it up, because, having no mother, they don't know how dangerous 'tis to eat rich, damp cake. They will die!

Smee (*fascinated*) It is the wickedest, prettiest policy ever I heard of.

Hook (*meaning well*) Shake hands on't.

Smee No, Captain, no.

He has to link with the hook, but he does not join in the song.

Hook

> Yo ho, yo ho, when I say 'paw'
> By fear they're overtook
> Naught's left upon your bones when you
> Have shaken hands with Hook!

Hook/Smee

> Yo ho, yo ho, when I say 'paw' . . .

Frightened by a tug at his hand, SMEE *is joining in the chorus when another sound stills them both. It is a tick, tick as of a clock, whose significance* HOOK *is, naturally, the first to recognize.*

Hook The Crocodile!

HOOK *totters from the scene.* SMEE *follows. A huge* CROCODILE, *of one thought compact, passes across the stage, ticking, and oozes after them.*

Storyteller The wood is now so silent, you may be sure it is full of redskins.

Enter TIGER LILY, *her ear to the ground, closely followed by the rest of the* PICCANINNY TRIBE, *snaking their way silently across the forest floor.*

Storyteller This is Tiger Lily, the princess of the Piccaninny tribe, whose braves would all have her to wife but she wards them off with a hatchet. Next is Clap of Thunder, then Lone Wolf, Dashing Deer, Running Water, Baby Bear, Shooting Star and Soft Cloud.

Enter GREAT BIG LITTLE PANTHER, *a magnificent and terrifying Indian brave, in the Fenimore Cooper story manner.*

Storyteller Last of all is Great Big Little Panther, a brave of so many scalps that they somewhat impede his progress.

Suddenly, at a signal from TIGER LILY, *the whole* TRIBE *freezes, as still as totem poles.*

Far away, across the lagoon, one of Smee's knuckles cracks!

Tiger Lily Pirates!

The Tribe Pirates!

They do not draw their knives. The knives slip into their hands.

Tiger Lily Have um scalps! What say Great Big Little Panther?

Panther Scalp um, oho, velly quick.

The Tribe (*in collaboration*) Scalp um, oho, velly quick. Ugg, ugg ... wah!

A fire is lit and they dance around and over it till they seem part of the leaping flames. TIGER LILY *invokes the spirits of war, the pipe of peace is broken; the* TRIBE *crawls off like a long snake that has not fed for many moons. Emerging from his tree,* TOOTLES *peers after the tail and summons the other boys, who issue from their holes.*

Tootles They are gone.

Slightly (*almost losing confidence in himself*) I do wish Peter was here.

First Twin H'sh! What is that? (*He is gazing at the lagoon and shrinks back.*)

Second Twin It is wolves, and they are chasing Nibs!

The baying WOLVES *are upon them quicker than any boy can scuttle down his tree.*

Nibs (*falling among his comrades*) Save me, save me!

Tootles What should we do?

Second Twin What would Peter do?

Curly Peter would look at them through his legs.

Slightly (*a brilliant suggestion*) Let us do what Peter would do!

The BOYS *advance backwards, looking between their legs at the snarling red-eyed enemy, who trot away foiled.*

First Twin (*swaggering*) We have saved you, Nibs. Did you see the pirates?

Nibs (*sitting up and agreeably aware that the centre of interest is now to pass to him*) No, but I saw a wonderfuller thing, Twin.

All mouths open for the information to be dropped into them.

High over the lagoon I saw the loveliest great white bird. It is flying this way.

They search the firmament.

Tootles What kind of a bird, do you think?

Nibs (*awed*) I don't know; but it looked so weary, and as it flies it moans 'Poor Wendy'.

First Twin (*who is perched on a high branch*) See, it comes, the Wendy.

They all see it now, and it is, of course, WENDY *herself, fluttering wearily among the tree-tops in her white nightgown.*

How white it is!

A dot of white is pursuing the 'Wendy' malignantly.

Tootles That is Tinker Bell. Tink is trying to hurt the Wendy. (*He makes a cup of his hands and calls*) Hullo, Tink!

A response from TINKER BELL *comes down in the fairy language.*

Tootles She says Peter wants us to shoot the Wendy.

Nibs Let us do what Peter wishes.

Slightly Ay, shoot it; quick, bows and arrows.

Tootles (*first with his bow*) Out of the way, Tink; I'll shoot it.

His bolt goes home and WENDY *falls straight to earth. No one could be more proud than* TOOTLES.

Tootles I have shot the Wendy; Peter will be so pleased.

Tink (*from some tree on which she is roosting comes the tinkle we can now translate as . . .*) You silly ass.

TOOTLES *falters.*

Tootles Why do you say that?

TINK *laughs maliciously. The other* BOYS *feel that* TOOTLES *may have blundered, and draw away from him.*

Slightly (*examining the fallen one more minutely*) This is no bird; I think it must be a lady.

Nibs (*who would have preferred it to be a bird*) And Tootles has killed her.

Curly Now I see, Peter was bringing her to us.

The BOYS *wonder for what object.*

Second Twin To take care of us?

Undoubtedly for some diverting purpose.

Boys (*though every one of them had wanted to have a shot at her*) Oh, Tootles!

Tootles (*gulping*) I did it. When ladies used to come to me in dreams I said 'Pretty mother', but when she really came I shot her!

He perceives the necessity of a solitary life for him.

Friends, goodbye.

Several Boys (*not very enthusiastic*) Don't go.

Tootles I must; I am so afraid of Peter.

He has gone a step or two toward oblivion when he is stopped by a crowing as of some victorious cock.

Boys Peter!

They make a paling of themselves in front of WENDY *as* PETER *skims around the tree-tops and reaches earth.*

Peter Greetings, boys! (*Their silence chafes him*) I am back; why do you not cheer? Great news, boys, I have brought at last the thing we have all been waiting for, a mother for us all!

Slightly (*vaguely*) Ay, ay.

Peter Have you not seen her? She flew this way.

Second Twin Oh mournful day!

Tootles (*after making a break in the paling*) Peter, I will show her to you.

Others (*closing the gap*) No, no.

Tootles (*majestically*) Stand back, all, and let Peter see.

The paling dissolves, and PETER *sees* WENDY *prone on the ground.*

Peter Wendy, with an arrow in her heart! (*He plucks it out*) Wendy is dead.

He is not so much pained as puzzled.

Curly I thought it was only flowers that die.

Peter Perhaps she is frightened at being dead?

None of them can say as to that.

Whose arrow?

Not one of them looks at TOOTLES.

Tootles Mine, Peter.

Peter (*raising the arrow as a dagger*) Oh dastard hand!

Tootles (*kneeling and bearing his breast*) Strike, Peter; strike true.

Peter (*undergoing a singular experience*) I cannot strike; there is something stays my hand.

In fact WENDY's *arm has risen.*

Nibs 'Tis she, the Wendy lady. See, her arm. (*To help a friend*) I think she said 'Poor Tootles.'

Peter (*investigating*) She lives!

The delightful feeling that they have been cleverer than they thought comes over them and they applaud themselves.

(*Holding up a button that is attached to her chain*) See, the arrow struck against this. It is a kiss I gave her; it has saved her life.

Slightly I remember kisses; let me see it. (*He takes it in his hand*) Ay, that is a kiss.

Peter Wendy, get better quickly and I'll take you to see the mermaids. She is awfully anxious to see a mermaid.

TINKER BELL, *who may have been off visiting her relations, returns to the wood and, under the impression that Wendy has been got rid of, is whistling as gaily as a canary. She is not wholly heartless, but is so small that she has only room for one feeling at a time.*

Curly Listen to Tink rejoicing because she thinks the Wendy is dead! (*Regardless of spoiling another's pleasure*) Tink, the Wendy lives.

TINK *gives expression to fury.*

Second Twin (*tell-tale*) It was she who said you wanted us to shoot the Wendy.

Peter She said that? Then listen, Tink, I am your friend no more.

There is a note of acerbity in TINK's *reply; it may mean 'Who wants you?'*

Peter Begone from me for ever.

Tink But, Peter . . .

Now it is a very wet tinkle.

Curly She is crying.

Tink ... I'm your *fairy*.

Tootles She says she is your fairy.

Peter (*who knows they are not worth worrying about*) Oh well, not for ever, but for a whole week.

TINK *goes off sulking, no doubt with an impression of giving all her friends an entirely false impression of* WENDY's *appearance.*

Peter Now what shall we do with Wendy?

Curly Let us carry her down into the house.

Slightly Ay, that is what one does with ladies.

Peter No, you must not touch her; it wouldn't be sufficiently respectful.

Slightly That is what I was thinking.

Tootles But if she lies there she will die.

Slightly Ay, there she will die. It is a pity, but there is no way out.

Peter Yes, there is. Let us build a house around her!

Cheers again, meaning that no difficulty baffles Peter.

Leave all to me. Bring the best of what we have. Gut our house. Be sharp.

They race down their trees. While Peter is engrossed in measuring WENDY *so that the house may fit her,* JOHN *and* MICHAEL, *who have probably landed on the island with a bump, wander forward, so draggled and tired that if you were to ask* MICHAEL *whether he is awake or asleep he would probably answer 'I haven't tried yet.'*

Michael (*bewildered*) John, wait for me!

John (*with the help of one eye but not always the same eye*) Come on, Michael, this must be the top. (*Thankfully*) Look, there is Peter. Peter, is this the place?

PETER, *alas, has already forgotten them, as soon maybe he will forget Wendy. The first thing she should do now that she is here is to sew a handkerchief for him, and knot it as a jog to his memory.*

Peter (*curtly*) Yes.

Michael Where is Wendy?

PETER *points.*

John (*who still wears his hat*) She is asleep.

Michael John, let us wake her and get her to make supper for us.

The BOYS *emerge, with odd articles of useless furniture and knick-knackery.*

John, look at them!

Peter (*still house-building*) Curly, see that these boys help in the building of the house.

John Build a house?

Curly For the Wendy.

John (*feeling that there must be some mistake here*) For Wendy? Why, she is only a girl.

Curly That is why we are her servants.

John (*dazed*) Are you Wendy's servants?

Peter Yes, and you also. Away with them.

In another moment they are woodsmen hacking at trees, with CURLY *as overseer.*

Peter Slightly, fetch a doctor. All look the other way.

SLIGHTLY *reels and goes, deftly removing* JOHN's *hat en passant.*

Michael What's he to do?

Tootles Gone for the doctor.

John A real doctor?

Nibs H'sh.

Slightly *returns professionally in John's hat.*

Peter Please, sir, are you a doctor?

Slightly (*trembling in his desire to give satisfaction*) Yes, my little man.

Peter Please, sir, a lady lies very ill.

Slightly (*taking care not to fall over her*) Tut, tut, where does she lie?

Peter In yonder glade.

It is a variation of a game they play.

Slightly I will put a glass thing in her mouth.

He inserts a pretend thermometer in WENDY's *mouth and gives it a moment to record its verdict.*

Tootles Oh dear, I hope she is not no more.

SLIGHTLY *shakes the thermometer and then consults it.*

Peter (*anxiously*) How is she?

Slightly Tut, tut, this has cured her.

Peter (*leaping joyously*) I am glad.

Slightly Give her beef tea out of a cup with a spout to it, tut, tut. I will call again in the morning. Good evening.

Peter Good evening.

All (*very politely*) Good evening.

SLIGHTLY *goes.*

John It was Slightly, wasn't it?

Tootles (*indicating* Peter) H'sh.

John Oh, I'm not afraid of *him*.

Peter What did you say, John?

John Nothing.

Slightly (*reappearing and lightly replacing the hat on* JOHN's *head*) Has the doctor been?

Totles Yes.

Slightly I'm sorry I missed him.

John (*still trying to catch up*) But . . .

PETER *surveys the odd bits and pieces the boys have brought up from below.*

Peter (*with an already fading recollection of the Darling nursery*) These are not good enough for Wendy. How I wish I knew the kind of house she would prefer!

First Twin Peter, she is moving in her sleep.

Tootles (*opening* WENDY's *mouth and gazing down into the depths*) Lovely!

Peter Perhaps she's going to sing in her sleep. Oh, Wendy, if only you could sing the kind of house you would like to have.

As if she had heard him and without opening her eyes, WENDY *starts to sing.*

Wendy
>If I had a little house
>It would be as small as small

As she sings, PETER *and the* BOYS *pay careful attention, preparing themselves to follow her instructions to the letter.*

>Little branches from the trees
>Would be made into a wall
>With a window in each one
>Just enough to see the sun.

The BOYS *sing as they start to build a house around* WENDY, *knocking down trees, laying a foundation and putting up the walls and the door-frame.*

Boys
>If I had a little house
>It would be as small as small
>Little branches from the trees
>Would be made into a wall
>With a window in each one
>Just enough to see the sun.

By the time the BOYS *have finished their verse, such is the urgency of* PETER's *silent orders,* WENDY *is nearly hidden from view.*

Wendy

> That would make my little house
> Quite the nicest ever seen
> With its windows painted bright –

Peter (*whispering*) Windows!

CURLY *rushes them in.*

Wendy

> – And its roof of mossy green.

Peter Roof!

Twins Roof! Roof!

And the TWINS *start to build the roof.*

Wendy

> And, I should have said before
> Roses growing round the door.

TOOTLES *goes out in search of roses as all the* BOYS *sing the second verse, building as they sing.*

Boys

> That would make my little house
> Quite the nicest ever seen
> With its windows painted bright
> And its roof of mossy green
> And, I should have said before
> Roses growing round the door.

Peter Roses!

Boys (*all of them now in charge*) Roses!

TOOTLES *arrives breathless with a festoon for the door.*

Thus springs into existence the most delicious little house for beginners.

First Twin I think it is finished.

Peter There is no chimney; we must have a chimney.

They await his deliberations anxiously.

John (*unwisely critical*) It certainly does need a chimney.

PETER *seizes* JOHN's *hat, knocks the top off it and places it on the roof. In the friendliest way smoke begins to come out of the hat.*

Peter All look your best; the first impression is awfully important.

The BOYS *all line up outside the door and attempt to smarten themselves up, though they don't really know how to do it.* PETER *knocks, and after a dreadful moment of suspense, in which they cannot help wondering if anyone is inside, the door opens and who should come out but* WENDY! *She has evidently been tidying up a little. She is quite surprised to find that she has nine children.*

Wendy (*genteelly*) Where am I?

Slightly Wendy lady, for you we built this house.

Nibs/Tootles Oh, say you are pleased.

Wendy (*stroking the pretty thing*) Lovely, darling house!

First Twin And we are your children.

Wendy (*affecting surprise*) Oh?

All (*kneeling with outstretched arms*) Wendy lady, be our mother!

Now that they know it is pretend they acclaim her greedily.

Wendy (*not to make herself too cheap*) Ought I? Of course it is frightfully fascinating; but you see I am only a little girl; I have no real experience.

Tootles That doesn't matter. What we sorely need is just a nice motherly person.

Wendy Oh dear, I feel that is just exactly what I am.

All (*severally*) It is, it is, we saw it at once.

Wendy Very well then, I will do my best.

In their glee they go dancing obstreperously round the little house, and she sees she must be firm with them as well as kind.

Come inside at once, you naughty children, I am sure your feet are damp. And before I put you to bed and tuck you in, I have just time to finish the story of *Cinderella*.

They all troop into the enchanting house, whose not least remarkable feature is that it holds them. The last one to go in is WENDY, *who pauses briefly before she enters. The* STORYTELLER *enters with* LIZA, *the Darlings' servant.*

Before Wendy went to sleep that night, for some strange reason she remembered Liza . . .

LIZA *moves across the island, examining the little house.*

Storyteller . . . who, of course, has no right to be here at all. But she has so few pleasures and is so young that we should just let her have a peep at the little house, so cozy and safe with a bright light showing through the window.

LIZA *goes.* PETER *comes out, and marches up and down with drawn sword.*

Storyteller Peter kept watch outside that night, for the pirates could be heard carousing far away on the lagoon and the wolves were on the prowl.

PETER *sits down, leaning against the door of the little house.*

Storyteller After a time he fell asleep ...

A horde of FAIRIES *crosses the island, giggling and singing, amongst them* TINKER BELL.

... and some unsteady fairies had to climb over him on their way home from an orgy. Any other child in their way they would have mischiefed, but they just tweaked Peter's nose and passed on.

The FAIRIES *disappear and on our last sight of* PETER *it is so dark that we just guess he is the little figure who has fallen asleep by the door.*

ACT THREE

The Mermaids' Lagoon

Storyteller From that night on, adventure became a daily occurrence. The best we can do is to show you one of them, as a specimen of an average hour on the island. The difficulty is – which adventure to choose. Should we take the brush with the redskins at Slightly Gulch? (*Soliciting preferences from members of the audience*) Or Tiger Lily and the Mermaids' Lagoon? Or Peter's defiance of the lions? Or the tale of the rich damp cake?

Members of the audience express their preferences, some politely, some not quite so politely.

Perhaps the best way would be to toss for it. (*He tosses a coin*) The Mermaids' Lagoon has won!

Demonstrations of disappointment or cynicism are waved aside as the lagoon appears.

It is the end of a long, playful day on the lagoon. The sun's rays have persuaded him to give them another five minutes for one more race over the waters before he gathers them up and lets in the moon.

There are many MERMAIDS *here going plop-plop, and one might attempt to count the tails did they not flash and disappear so quickly. At times a lovely girl leaps in the air seeking to get rid of her excess of scales, which fall in a silver shower as she shakes them off. From the coral grottoes beneath the lagoon, where are the mermaids' bedchambers, comes fitful music. One of the most bewitching of these blue-eyed creatures*

74

is lying lazily on marooners' rock, combing her long tresses and noting effects in a transparent shell. PETER, WENDY, *and the* BOYS *are in the water behind the rock. They have tracked this* MERMAID *as if she were a trout, and at a signal ten pairs of arms come whack upon the* MERMAID *to enclose her. Alas, this is only what was meant to happen, for she hears the signal (*PETER's *cock-crow) and slips through their arms into the water. It has been such a near thing that there are scales on some of their hands. They climb on to the rock crestfallen.*

Wendy (*preserving her scales as carefully as if they were rare postage stamps*) I did so want to catch a mermaid.

Peter (*getting rid of his*) It is awfully difficult to catch a mermaid.

The mermaids at times find it just as difficult to catch him, though he sometimes joins them in their own game, which is lazily blowing their bubbles into the air and seeing who can catch them. The number of bubbles Peter has flown away with! When the weather grows cold, mermaids migrate to the other side of the world, and he once went with a great shoal of them half the way.

Peter They are such cruel creatures, Wendy, that they try to pull boys and girls like you into the water and drown them.

Wendy (*too guarded by this time to ask what he means precisely by 'like you' though she is very desirous of knowing*) How hateful!

She is slightly different in appearance now, rather rounder, while JOHN *and* MICHAEL *are not quite so round. The reason is that when new lost children arrive at his underground home Peter finds new trees for them to go down by, and instead of fitting the tree to them he makes them fit the tree. Sometimes it can be done by adding or removing garments, but if you are too bumpy, or the tree is an odd shape, he has things done to you with a roller, and after that you fit.*

John (*clambering on to the rock*) Doesn't it seem odd, swimming around in one's clothes?

Peter No, just like dogs.

He plunges in, followed by JOHN *and then* WENDY. *The other* BOYS *start playing King of the Castle, throwing each other into the water, taking headers and so on, while* PETER *and* WENDY *climb back on to the rock and continue their conversation.*

Peter Wendy, this is a fearfully important rock. It is called Marooners' Rock. Sailors are marooned, you know, when their captain leaves them on a rock and sails away.

Wendy Leaves them on this little rock to drown?

Peter (*lightly*) Oh, they don't live long. Their hands are tied, so that they can't swim. When the tide is full, this rock is covered with water, and then the sailor drowns.

Wendy How awful!

WENDY *is uneasy as she surveys the rock, which is the only one in the lagoon, and no larger than a table. Since she last looked around a threatening change has come over the scene. The sun has gone, but the moon has not come. What has come is a cold shiver across the waters which has sent all the wiser mermaids to their coral recesses. They know that evil is creeping over the lagoon. Of the boys* PETER *is, of course, the first to scent it, and he has leapt to his feet before the words strike the rock.*

Starkey/Smee
> Avast, belay, yo ho, heave to
> A-pirating we go
> And if we're parted by a shot
> We're sure to meet below.

The games on the rock and around it end so abruptly that several divers are checked in the air. There they hang waiting for the word of command from PETER . . .

Peter Pirates!

. . . *and when they get it they strike the water simultaneously, and the rock is at once as bare as if suddenly they had been blown off it. Thus the* PIRATES *find it deserted when their dinghy strikes the rock and is nearly stove in by the concussion.*

Smee Luff, you spalpeen, luff!

They are SMEE *and* STARKEY, *with* TIGER LILY, *their captive, bound hand and foot.*

Smee What we have to do is hoist the redskin on to the rock and leave her there to drown.

To one of her race this is an end darker than death by fire or torture, for it is written in the laws of the Piccaninnies that there is no path through water to the happy hunting ground.

Storyteller The face of Tiger Lily is impassive; she is the daughter of a chief . . .

Starkey (*chagrined because she does not mewl*) No mewling. This is your reward for prowling around the ship with a knife in your mouth.

Storyteller ... and as a chief's daughter she must die. It is enough.

Tiger Lily (*stoically*) Enough said.

Smee (*who would have preferred a farewell palaver*) So that's it!

Starkey (*experiencing for perhaps the last time the stirrings of a man*) Not so rough, Smee; roughish, but not so rough.

Smee (*dragging her on to the rock*) It is the Captain's orders.

A stave has in some time past been driven into the rock, probably to mark the burial place of hidden treasure, and to this they moor the dinghy.

Wendy (*in the water*) Poor Tiger Lily!

Starkey What was that?

WENDY *and the* BOYS *bob under the water.*

Peter (*who can imitate the Captain's voice so perfectly that even the author has a dizzy feeling that at times he was really Hook*) Ahoy there, you lubbers!

Starkey It is the Captain; he must be swimming out to us.

Smee (*calling*) We have put the redskin on the rock, Captain.

Peter Set her free.

Smee But, Captain ...

Peter Cut her bonds, or I'll plunge my hook in you.

Smee This is queer!

Starkey (*unmanned*) Let us follow the Captain's orders.

They undo the thongs and TIGER LILY *slides between their legs into the lagoon, forgetting in her haste to utter her war cry, but* PETER *utters if for her, so naturally that even the boys are deceived. It is at that moment that the voice of the true* HOOK *is heard.*

Hook Boat ahoy!

Smee (*relieved*) It is the Captain.

HOOK *is swimming, and they help him to scale the rock. He is in a gloomy mood.*

Starkey Captain, is all well?

Smee He sighs.

Starkey He sighs again.

Smee (*counting*) And yet a third time he sighs. (*With foreboding*) What's up, Captain?

Hook (*who perhaps has found the rich damp cake untouched*) The game is up. Those boys have found a mother!

Starkey Oh evil day!

Smee What is a mother?

Wendy (*horrified*) He doesn't know!

Hook (*sharply*) What was that?

PETER *makes the splash of a mermaid's tail.*

Starkey One of them mermaids.

Hook Dost not know, Smee? A mother is ...

He finds it more difficult to explain than he had expected, and looks about him for an illustration. He finds one in a great

NEVER BIRD *which drifts past in a nest as large as the roomiest basin.*

There is a lesson in mothers for you! The nest must have fallen into the water, but would the bird desert her eggs?

PETER, *who is now more or less off his head, makes the sound of the* NEVER BIRD *answering in the negative.*

Peter No, I wouldn't.

Hook No, she wouldn't.

Smee (*not usually a man of ideas*) Captain, could we not capture these boys' mother and make her our mother?

Hook O ... besity and bunions! 'Tis a princely scheme. We will seize the children, make them walk the plank, and Wendy shall be our mother!

Wendy Never!

Another splash from PETER. *The* PIRATES *listen for a moment.*

Hook, Smee *and* **Starkey** Mermaids!

Hook What say you, bullies?

Smee There is my hand on't.

Starkey And mine.

Hook And there is my hook. (*All swear,* SMEE *and* STARKEY *somewhat gingerly in view of the hook*) But I had forgot; where is the redskin?

Smee (*shaken*) That is all right, Captain; we let her go.

Hook (*terrible*) Let her go?

Smee 'Twas your own orders, Captain.

Starkey (*whimpering*) You called over the water to us to let her go.

Hook Brimstone and gall, what cozening is here? (*Disturbed by their faithful faces*) Lads, I gave no such order.

Smee 'Tis passing queer.

Hook (*addressing the immensities*) Spirit that haunts this dark lagoon tonight, dost hear me?

Peter (*in the same voice*) Odds, bobs, hammer and tongs, I hear you.

Hook (*gripping the stave for support*) Who are you, stranger, speak.

Peter (*who is only too ready to speak*) I am James Hook, Captain of the Jolly Roger.

Hook (*now white to the gills*) No, no you are not.

Peter Brimstone and gall, say that again and I'll cast anchor in you.

Hook If you are Hook, come tell me, who am I?

Peter A codfish, only a codfish.

Hook (*aghast*) A codfish?

Smee (*drawing back from him*) Have we been captained all this time by a codfish?

Starkey It's lowering to our pride.

Hook (*feeling that his ego is slipping from him*) Don't desert me, bullies.

Peter (*top-heavy*) Fishy, fishy, fishy!

There is a touch of the feminine in HOOK, *as in all the greatest pirates, and it prompts him to try the guessing game.*

Hook Have you another name?

Peter (*falling to the lure*) Ay, ay.

Hook (*thirstily*) Vegetable?

Peter No.

Hook Mineral?

Peter No.

Hook Animal?

Peter (*after a hurried consultation with* TOOTLES) Yes.

Hook Man?

Peter (*with scorn*) No.

Hook Boy?

Peter Yes.

Hook Ordinary boy?

Peter No!

Hook Wonderful boy?

Peter (*to* WENDY's *distress*) Yes!

Hook Are you in England?

Peter No.

Hook Are you here?

Peter Yes.

Hook (*beaten, though he feels he has very nearly got it*) Smee, you ask him some questions.

Smee (*rummaging his brains*) I can't think of a thing.

Peter Can't guess, can't guess! (*Foundering in his cockiness*) Do you give it up?

Hook Yes.

Peter All of you?

Smee, Starkey *and* **Hook** Yes!

Peter (*crowing*) Well, then, I am Peter Pan! (*Now they have him*)

Hook Pan! Smee, into the water. Starkey, mind the boat. Take him dead or alive!

Peter (*who still has all his baby teeth*) Boys, lam into the pirates!

For a moment, the only two we can see are in the dinghy, where JOHN *throws himself on* STARKEY. STARKEY *wriggles into the lagoon and* JOHN *leaps so quickly after him that he reaches it first. The impression left on* STARKEY *is that he is being attacked by the* TWINS. *The water becomes stained. Here and there a head shows in the water. In the growing gloom, some strike at their friends,* SLIGHTLY *getting* TOOTLES *in the fourth rib while he is being pinked by* CURLY. *It looks as if the boys are getting the worst of it, which is perhaps just as well at this point, because* PETER, *who will be the determining factor in the end, has a perplexing way of changing sides if he is winning too easily.* STARKEY *and* SMEE, *out-numbered and badly shaken, swim for the shore.*

HOOK's *iron claw makes a circle of black water around him from which the boys flee like fishes, clambering aboard the abandoned dinghy and rowing to safety. There is only one prepared to enter that dreadful circle. His name is* PAN. HOOK *has risen to the rock to breathe, and at the same moment* PETER *scales it on the opposite side. The rock is now wet and slippery as a ball, and they have to crawl rather than climb. Suddenly they are face to face.* PETER *gnashes his pretty teeth with joy. Quick as thought he snatches a knife from* HOOK's *belt and is about to drive it home, when he sees he is higher up the rock than his foe.*

Hook Bad form!

PETER *offers the pirate a helping hand.* HOOK *takes it gratefully – and then bites it. Not the pain of this but its unfairness is what dazes* PETER. *It makes him quite helpless. Every child is affected thus the first time he is treated unfairly. All he thinks he has a right to when he comes to you to be yours is fairness. After you have been unfair to him, he will love you again, but will never afterwards be quite the same boy. No one ever gets over the first unfairness; no one except* PETER. *He often meets it but he always forgets it. That was the real difference between him and all the rest. So when he meets it now it is like the first time and he can only stand and stare, horrified.*

HOOK *seizes the advantage and claws twice.* PETER *is untouched, but in his bewilderment he rolls off the rock.* HOOK *is triumphant, but not for long, for the* CROCODILE, *whose tick has been drowned in the strife, suddenly rears its jaws, and* HOOK, *who has almost stepped into them, is pursued by it to land.*

All is quiet on the lagoon now, not a sound save little waves nibbling at the rock, which is smaller than when we last looked at it, and faraway cries of 'Peter – Wendy' from the boys in the dinghy, whose hearts would sink if they knew of the peril of Wendy and her Captain.

These two small figures are now on the rock, but they have fainted. A MERMAID who has dared to come back into the stillness stretches up her arms and is slowly pulling WENDY into the water to drown her. WENDY starts up just in time.

Wendy Peter! (*He rouses himself and looks around him*) Where are we, Peter?

Peter We are on the rock, but it is getting smaller. Soon the water will be over it. Listen!

They can hear the wash of the relentless little waves as the rock gets smaller.

Wendy We must go.

Peter Yes.

Wendy Shall we swim or fly?

Peter Wendy, do you think you could swim or fly to the island without me?

Wendy You know I couldn't, Peter; I am just a beginner.

Peter Hook wounded me twice.

He believes it; he is so good at pretending that he feels the pain, his arms hang limp.

I can neither swim nor fly.

Wendy Do you mean that we shall both be drowned?

Peter Look how the water is rising!

They cover their faces with their hands as the rock gets even smaller. Then something touches WENDY *as lightly as a kiss.*

(*With little interest*) It must be the tail of the kite we made for Michael; you remember, it tore itself out of his hands and floated away.

He looks up and sees the kite sailing overhead.

The kite! Why shouldn't it carry you?

He grabs the tail and pulls, and the kite responds.

Wendy Both of us!

Peter It can't lift two. Michael and Curly tried.

She knows very well that if it can lift her it can lift him also, for she has been told by the boys as a deadly secret that one of the things about him is that he is no weight at all. But it is a forbidden subject.

Wendy I won't go without you. Let us draw lots which is to stay behind.

Peter And you a lady, never!

The tail is in her hands, and the kite is tugging hard.

Goodbye, Wendy!

Wendy (*as she rises upwards*) Peter!

The kite draws her out of sight across the lagoon. The STORYTELLER, *who has witnessed these extraordinary events just as we have, emerges into view at the top of the island.*

Storyteller Peter was alone on the lagoon. The waters rose still further, lapping over the rock, and he knew that it would soon be submerged. Pale rays of light tiptoed across the waters, and from the coral grottoes could be heard a sound, at once the most musical and the most melancholy in the world, the mermaids calling to the moon to rise.

PETER *is afraid at last, and a tremor runs through him, like a shudder passing over the lagoon. But on the lagoon, one shudder follows another till there are hundreds of them, and he feels just the one.*

Peter (*with a drum beating in his breast as if he were a real boy at last*) To die will be an awfully big adventure.

The lagoon is now suffused with moonlight. The water is over PETER's *feet. The nest is borne nearer, and the* NEVER BIRD, *after cooing a message to him, leaves it and sings her way upwards.* PETER, *who knows the bird language, slips into the nest, first removing the two eggs and placing them in Starkey's hat, which has been left on the stave. The hat drifts away from the rock, but he uses the stave as a mast. The wind is driving him towards the open sea. He takes off his shirt, which he had forgotten to remove while bathing, and unfurls it as a sail. His vessel tacks, and he passes from sight, victorious.*

Interval.

ACT FOUR

The Home Under The Ground

The STORYTELLER *appears in the wood above the underground home. All around him, the* PICCANINNY
TRIBE *sits in watchful stillness.*

Storyteller We have now reached the evening that was to
be known among the children as the Night of Nights,
because of its adventures and their upshot. What you can
see is the Home under the Ground with the children in it,
and the wood above ground with the redskins on it!
Below, the children are preparing their evening meal.
Above, the redskins are guarding the children from the
pirates. The only way of communication between these
two parties is by means of the hollow trees. Slightly, being
addicted when hot to the drinking of water, has swelled in
consequence, and secretly scooped his tree for easier
descent. I shall therefore use his.

The STORYTELLER *descends to the home under the ground.
The house has an earthen floor, which is handy for digging in
if you want to go fishing; and owing to there being so many
entrances there is not much wall space. The* CHILDREN *are
sitting around an invisible table, silently eating their equally
invisible food. They often have these suppers and like them on
occasion as well as the other kind. The pretend meals are not
Wendy's idea; indeed she was rather startled to find, on
arriving, that Peter knew of no other kind, and she is not
absolutely certain even now that he does eat the other kind,
though no one appears to do it more heartily. He insists that
the pretend meals should be partaken of with gusto, and so we*

see his band doing their best to obey orders. All the BOYS *except Peter are here, and* WENDY *has the head of the table, smiling complacently at their captivating ways, but doing her best at the same time to see that they keep the rules about hands-off-the-table, no-speaking-at-once, and so on. She is wearing romantic woodland garments, sewn by herself, with red berries in her hair which go charmingly with her complexion, as she knows; indeed she searched for red berries the morning after she reached the island. The* BOYS *are in picturesque attire of her contrivance, and if these don't always fit well, the fault is not hers but the wearers', for they constantly put on each other's things if they put on anything at all. Their seats are pumpkins or the large gay mushrooms of which we have seen an imitation one concealing the chimney. There is an enormous fireplace which is in almost any part of the room where you care to light it, and across this Wendy has stretched strings made of fibre, from which she hangs her washing. There are also various tomfool things in the room of no use whatever. Michael's basket bed is nailed high upon the wall as if to protect him from the cat, but there is no indication at present of where the others sleep.* MICHAEL *indeed, is in his basket at this moment, for Wendy insists on the correctness of always having a baby in the room on family occasions, and mealtimes are certainly family occasions. At the back between two of the tree trunks is a grindstone, and near it is a lovely hole, the size of a band-box, with a gay curtain drawn across it so that you cannot see what is inside. The* STORYTELLER *emerges from Slightly's tree, a little soiled from his descent, and approaches the tiny curtain.*

Storyteller This little niche is Tinker Bell's withdrawing room and bedchamber ... (*He peeks behind the curtain*) ... and it's just as well that you can't see inside, for everything is so exquisite that you could scarcely resist making off with something. (*Another peek*) The couch is a genuine Queen Mab, the mirror is a Puss-in-Boots, of which there are now only three, unchipped, known to the fairy dealers, and the chest-of-drawers ... (*He slips his hand into the niche and removes the said chest*) ... the chest-of-drawers is an authentic Charming the Sixth!

Tink (*swishing open the curtain*) Put that back!

Storyteller Oh ... I do beg your pardon.

He replaces the chest-of-drawers.

Tink Honestly!

The curtain closes with an angry flourish.

Storyteller (*rather sheepish*) Tink is within at present as one should have guessed from the glow, for though she has a chandelier from Tiddly and Wink's for the look of the thing, of course she lights her residence herself.

FIRST TWIN, *guilty of some awful lapse in manners, moves away from the table and sits on a high stool at the other side of the room.* WENDY, *following him, takes down a dunce's cap from the wall and puts it on his head.*

Storyteller The dunce's cap is an invention of Wendy's, but not wholly successful, because everybody wants to be dunce.

The CHILDREN *continue with their imaginary meal.*

Normally their suppers consist chiefly of bread-fruit, tappa-rolls, yams, mammee apples, and banana splash, washed down with calabashes of poe-poe. But it is a pretend meal this evening, with nothing whatsoever on the table.

The meal suddenly erupts into hilarity and mayhem.

Wendy (*her fingers to her ears, for their chatter and clatter are deafening*) Si-lence! Is your mug empty, Slightly?

Slightly (*who would not say this if he had a mug*) Not quite empty, thank you.

Nibs Mummy, he has not even begun to drink his poe-poe.

Slightly (*seizing his chance, for this is tale-bearing*) I complain of Nibs!

JOHN *holds up his hand.*

Wendy Well, John?

John (*indicating the largest and only vacant pumpkin*) May I sit in Peter's chair as he is not here?

Wendy In your father's chair? Certainly not.

John He is not really our father. He did not even know how to be a father till I showed him.

Second Twin (*at this is insubordination*) I complain of John!

The gentle TOOTLES raises his hand.

Tootles (*who has the poorest opinion of himself*) I don't suppose Michael would let me be baby?

Michael No, I won't.

Tootles May I be dunce?

First Twin (*from his perch*) No. It's awfully difficult to be dunce.

Tootles As I can't do anything important would any of you like to see me do a trick?

All No.

Tootles (*subsiding*) I hadn't really any hope.

Nibs (*the tale-telling breaks out again*) Slightly is coughing on the table.

Curly The twins began with tappa-rolls.

Slightly I complain of Nibs!

Nibs I complain of Slightly!

Wendy (*with that warning note that tells the boys they may be pushing her too far*) Oh dear, I am sure I sometimes think that spinsters are to be envied.

Michael Wendy, I am too big for a cradle.

The BOYS *make a rush for the cradle, vying with one another to take* MICHAEL's *place.*

Wendy (*firm but kind*) You are the littlest, and a cradle is such a nice homely thing to have about a house. You others can clear away.

The BOYS *clear away with dispatch, washing dishes they don't have in a non-existent sink and stowing them in a cupboard that isn't there. A movement of the* INDIANS *draws our attention to the scene above. Hitherto, with the exception of* PANTHER, *who sits on guard on top of the little house, they have been hunkering in their blankets, mute but picturesque; now all rise and prostrate themselves before the majestic figure of* PETER, *who approaches through the forest carrying a gun and game bag. It is not exactly a gun. He often wanders away alone with this weapon, and when he comes back you are never absolutely certain whether he has had an adventure or not. He may have forgotten about it so completely that he says nothing about it; and then when you go out you find the body. On the other hand he may say a great deal about it, and tells* WENDY, *as a thing of no importance, that he got these marks from the little people for cheeking them at a fairy wedding, and she listens politely, but she is never quite sure, you know; indeed the only one who is sure about anything on the island is* PETER.

Peter The Great White Father is glad to see the Piccaninny braves protecting his wigwam from the pirates.

Tiger Lily The Great White Father save me from pirates. Me his velly nice friend now; no let pirates hurt him.

Braves Ugg, ugg, wah!

TIGER LILY *takes* PETER *aside.*

Tiger Lily Now we rub noses.

Peter (*grudgingly*) Oh, all right.

Tiger Lily (*the rubbing of noses inflaming her tender feelings*) Tiger Lily wants to be your Wendy. Peter Paleface come with me. Be Great Indian White Chief and this your squaw.

Peter Desert Wendy – never!

Tiger Lily (*the mention of that name*) Me scalp you if you no nice to me.

Peter I don't care, Wendy is my only mother.

Tiger Lily (*withdrawing into a haughty splendour*) Tiger Lily has spoken.

Panther (*not approving of all this, but he must stick up for the princess*) Loola, loola! Great Big Little Panther has spoken!

Lone Wolf (*following suit*) Lone Wolf has spoken!

The rest of THE TRIBE *try to add their voices and their names to the oath but are sharply cut off by* PETER.

Peter The Great White Father has spoken! And now shut up!

He descends his tree, not unheard by WENDY.

Wendy Children, I hear your father's step. He likes you to meet him at the door.

PETER *scatters pretend nuts among them and watches sharply to see that they crunch with relish.*

All Nuts!

Wendy Peter, you just spoil them, you know!

John (*who would be incredulous if he dared*) Any sport, Peter?

Peter Two tigers and a pirate.

John (*boldly*) Where are their heads?

Peter (*contracting his little brows*) In the bag.

John But... (*No, he doesn't say it. He backs away*)

Wendy (*peeping into the bag*) They are beauties! (*She has learned her lesson*)

First Twin Father, we want to do the Spooky Dance.

Peter Dance away, my little men.

Twins But we want you to dance.

Peter Me, my old bones would rattle.

Curly And mummy too.

Wendy The mother of such an armful dance!

Slightly As it is Saturday night?

They have long lost count of the days, but always if they want to do anything special they say this is Saturday night, and then they do it.

Wendy Of course it is Saturday night, Peter?

Peter People of our figure, Wendy?

Wendy And it is only among our own progeny.

He shrugs an indifferent assent.

Peter True, true.

Wendy On with your nighties first.

They disappear into various recesses, and PETER *and* WENDY, *with her darning, are left by the fire to dodder parentally.*

Every heel with a hole in it. (*Beaming*) Dear Peter, with such a large family I have passed my best, but you don't want to change me, do you?

Peter (*uncomfortable*) No.

She is too loving not to know that he is not loving enough, and she hesitates as one who knows the answer to her question.

Wendy What is wrong, Peter?

Peter (*scared*) It is only pretend, isn't it, that I am their father?

Wendy (*drooping*) Oh yes.

His sigh of relief is without consideration for her feelings.

But they are ours, Peter, yours and mine.

Peter (*determined to get at facts, the only things that puzzle him*) But not really?

Wendy Not if you don't wish it.

Peter I don't.

Wendy (*knowing she ought not to probe but driven to it by something within*) What are your exact feelings for me, Peter?

Peter (*in the classroom*) Those of a devoted son, Wendy.

Wendy (*turning away*) I thought so.

Peter You are so puzzling. Tiger Lily is just the same; there is something or other she wants me to be, but she says it is not my mother.

Wendy (*with spirit*) No, indeed it isn't.

Peter Then what is it?

Wendy It isn't for a lady to tell.

Peter Perhaps Tink will tell me.

Wendy (*with spirit*) Oh yes, Tink will tell you. She has no scruples. She hugs you openly – Tink's an abandoned little creature.

The curtain of the fairy chamber opens slightly and TINK *who has been eavesdropping tinkles a laugh of scorn.*

Tink I know I am, and like a true woman, I glory in it.

Peter She says she knows she's an abandoned little creature and that like a true woman, she glories in it. (*Badgered*) I suppose that she wants to be my mother.

Tink You silly ass!

Wendy (*who has picked up some of the fairy words*) I almost agree with her!

The BOYS *all run in wearing their nightgowns and pyjamas, and the dance begins. Such a deliciously creepy dance it is, in which they pretend to be frightened at their own shadows; little witting that so soon shadows will close in upon them, from whom they will shrink in real fear. So uproariously gay is the dance, as they buffet each other on the bed and out of it!* FIRST TWIN *is the best dancer and performs mightily on the bed and in it and out of it and over it to an accompaniment of pillow fights by the less agile; and then there is a rush at* WENDY.

Nibs Now the story you promised to tell us as soon as we were in bed!

Wendy (*severely*) As far as I can see you are not in bed yet.

At last we see how they sleep, for in a babel the great bed which stands on end by day against the wall is unloosed from custody and lowered to the floor. Though large, it is a tight fit for so many BOYS, *and* WENDY *has made a rule that there is to be no turning round till one gives the signal, when all turn at once. They scramble into the bed and the effect is as a box full of sardines.*

Wendy (*drawing up her stool*) Well, there was once a gentleman.

Curly I wish he had been a lady.

PETER PAN**Nibs** I wish he had been a white rat.

Wendy You mustn't interrupt! There was a lady also...

First Twin Excuse my interrupting you, Mummy, but you say there was a lady. You mean that there *is* a lady also, don't you? (*Anxiously*) She's not dead, is she?

Wendy Oh no.

Tootles I'm awfully glad she's not dead. Are you glad, John?

John Of course I am.

Tootles Are you glad, Slightly?

Slightly Rather!

Tootles Are you glad, Twins?

Second Twin We are just glad.

Wendy The gentleman's name was Mr Darling and the lady's name was Mrs Darling...

John I knew them!

Michael (*who has been allowed to join in the circle*) I think I knew them.

Wendy They were married, you know; and what do you think they had?

Nibs White rats?

Wendy No, they had three descendants. White rats are descendants also. Almost everything is a descendant. Now these three children had a faithful nurse called Nana.

Michael (*alas*) What a funny name!

Wendy But Mr Darling – (*faltering*) or was it Mrs Darling –

was angry with her and chained her up in the yard; so all the children flew away. They flew away to the Never Land where the Lost Boys are.

Curly I just thought they did; I don't know how it is, but I just thought they did.

Tootles Oh, Wendy, was one of the Lost Boys called Tootles?

Wendy Yes, he was.

Tootles (*dazzled*) Am I in a story? Wendy, tell us what Tootles did, tell us what Tootles said, tell us what Tootles was like! Nibs, I am in a story.

Peter (*who is by the fire making Pan's pipes with his knife and is determined that* WENDY *shall have fair play, however beastly a story he may think it*) A little less noise there.

Wendy (*melting over the beauty of her present performance but without any real qualms*) Now I want you to consider the feelings of the unhappy parents with all their children flown away. Think, oh think, of the empty beds.

The heartless ones think of them with glee.

First Twin (*cheerfully*) It's awfully sad.

Wendy But our heroine knew that her mother would always leave the window open for her progeny to fly back by; so they stayed away for years and had a lovely time.

PETER *is interested at last.*

First Twin Did they ever go back?

Wendy (*comfortably*) Let us now take a peep into the future.

Years have rolled by, and who is this elegant lady of uncertain age alighting at London station?

The tension is unbearable.

Nibs Oh, Wendy, who is she?

Wendy (*swelling*) Can it be – yes – no – yes, it is the fair Wendy!

Tootles I am glad. Are you glad, Slightly?

Wendy Who are the two noble portly figures accompanying her, now grown to man's estate? Can they be John and Michael? They are. (*Pride of* MICHAEL) 'See, dear brothers,' says Wendy, pointing upward, 'there is the window standing open.' So they flew up to their loving parents, and pen cannot inscribe the happy scene over which we draw a veil.

Her triumph is spoiled by a groan from PETER *and she hurries to him.*

Peter, what is it? (*Thinking he is ill and looking lower than his chest*) What is it?

Peter It isn't that kind of pain. Wendy, you are wrong about mothers. I thought like you about the window, so I flew back, but the window was barred, for my mother had forgotten all about me and there was another little boy sleeping in my bed.

This is a general damper.

John Wendy, let us go home!

Wendy Are you sure mothers are like that?

Peter Yes.

Wendy John, Michael!

She clasps them to her.

Second Twin (*alarmed*) You are not to leave us, Wendy?

Wendy I must.

Nibs Not tonight?

Wendy I'm frightened to stay another moment. Peter, will you make the necessary arrangements? (*She asks it in the steely tones women adopt when they are prepared secretly for opposition*)

Peter (*coolly*) If you wish it.

He ascends his tree to give the INDIANS *their instructions. The* LOST BOYS *gather around* WENDY.

Tootles If there is anything we could do, Wendy, to make you more comfortable.

Curly We would darn our own stockings, Wendy.

Slightly We would build you a bigger house.

Wendy I love my little house!

First Twin It will be worse than before she came!

Slightly We shan't let her go!

Nibs Let's keep her prisoner.

First Twin Let's chain her.

Second Twin (*threatening*) Wendy, it's because we love you so.

Wendy (*with one of those inspirations women have, in an emergency, to make use of some male who need otherwise have no hope*) Tootles, I appeal to you.

Tootles (*leaping to his death if necessary*) I am just Tootles and nobody minds me much, but the first who does not behave to Wendy like an English gentleman, I will blood him severely. What are you, Slightly?

Slightly (*suddenly cowed*) English gentleman.

Tootles What are you, Nibs?

Nibs (*ditto*) English gentleman.

Tootles What are you, Curly?

Curly English gentleman.

Tootles What are you, Twins?

Twins English gentlemen.

Wendy (*dissolving all the violence into a fond embrace*) Dear, dear boys!

PETER *returns.*

Peter (*with awful serenity*) Wendy, I told the braves to guide you through the wood as flying tires you so.

Wendy Thank you, Peter.

Peter Then Tinker Bell will take you across the sea.

Tink (*a little twitch of the curtain*) And drop her into it!

Nibs (*approaching the chamber and using as much authority as he can muster*) Tink, you are to get up and take Wendy on a journey.

Tink (*from within*) Shan't!

Nibs (*star-eyed*) She says she won't!

PETER (*pulling aside the little curtain and addressing* TINK *directly*) If you don't get up, Tink . . . (*Closing the curtain and looking away, with a blush*) . . . and *dress* at once!

Tink (*to please him her only object*) All right, Peter.

Peter She is getting up!

Wendy (*quivering now that the time to depart has come*) Dear ones, if you will all come with me, I feel almost sure I can get my father and mother to adopt you.

There is joy at this, not that they want parents, but novelty is their religion.

Nibs But won't they think us rather a handful?

Wendy (*a swift reckoner*) Oh no, it will only mean having a few beds in the drawing-room; they can be hidden behind screens on first Thursdays.

Everything depends on PETER.

All Peter, may we go?

Peter (*carelessly through the pipes, to which he is giving a finishing touch*) All right.

They scurry off to dress for the adventure.

Wendy (*insinuatingly*) I'm going to give you your medicine before you go. Get your things, Peter.

Peter (*skipping about and playing fairy music on his pipes, the only music he knows*) I am not going with you.

Wendy Yes, Peter.

Peter No.

Wendy To find your mother.

Peter (*his pipes more riotous than ever*) I just want always to be a boy and to have fun.

The lost ones run back gaily, each one carrying a stick with a bundle on the end of it.

Wendy Peter isn't coming.

All the faces go blank.

John (*even* JOHN) Peter not coming!

Tootles (*overthrown*) Peter, why not?

CURLY *cries. There is a general fear that they are perhaps making the mistake of their lives.*

Peter Now then, no fuss, no blubbering. (*With dreadful cynicism*) I hope you like your mothers! Are you ready, Tink?

Tink (*emerging from her little chamber and tidily drawing the curtain behind her*) Aye, aye.

Peter Then lead the way.

TINK *darts up any tree, but she is the only one, for a terrible sound can be heard from above ground.*

Pirates
> Yo ho, yo ho, the pirate life,
> The flag of skull and bones,

Peter Pirates!

The PIRATES *creep into the wood above the underground home and slowly advance on the circle of* INDIANS.

Pirates
> A merry hour, a hempen rope . . .

The PIRATES *have now completely surrounded the* INDI-ANS, *who have known the pirate whereabouts since, early in the night, another one of Smee's fingers cracked. The brush-wood has closed behind their scouts as silently as the sand on the mole; for hours they have imitated the lonely call of the coyote; no stratagem has been overlooked, but alas, they have trusted to the pale-face's honour to await an attack at dawn, when his courage is known to be at its lowest ebb. The* STORYTELLER *arrives, breathless with his news.*

Storyteller Captain Hook has basely broken the two laws of Indian warfare, which are that the redskins should attack first and that it should be at dawn. If the braves would rise quickly they might still have time to scalp, but this they are forbidden to do by the traditions of their race, for it is written that they must never express surprise in the presence of the pale-face. Thus perish the flower of the Piccaninnies.

Pirates
     ... And hey for Davy Jones!

The air above is suddenly rent with shrieks and the clash of steel. Though they cannot see, the boys know that HOOK *and his crew are upon the* INDIANS. *Mouths open and remain open, all in mute appeal to* PETER. *He is the only boy on his feet now, a sword in his hand, the same he slew Barbecue with; and in his eye is the lust of battle. We can watch the carnage that is invisible to the children.* HOOK *falls upon the* INDIANS *pell-mell, and one cannot withhold a reluctant admiration for the wit that conceived so subtle a scheme and the fell genius with which it is carried out. Many of the* INDIANS *are slain, though not unavenged, for with* LONE WOLF *fall* ALF MASON *and* CANARY ROBB, *while other pirates to bite the dust are* BLACK GILMOUR *and* ALAN HERB. CHAY TURLEY *is tomahawked by* PAN-THER, *who eventually cuts a way through the shambles with* TIGER LILY *and a remnant of the* TRIBE. *This onslaught passes and is gone like a fierce wind.*

The victors wipe their cutlasses, and squint, ferret-eyed, at their leader. He remains, as ever, aloof in spirit and in substance. He signs to them to descend the trees, for he is convinced that PAN *is down there, and though he has smoked the bees it is the honey he wants. There is something in* PETER *that at all times goads this extraordinary man to frenzy; it is the boy's cockiness, which disturbs* HOOK *like an insect. If you have seen a lion in a cage futilely pursuing a sparrow you will know what is meant. The* PIRATES *try to do their Captain's bidding, but the apertures prove to be not wide enough for them;* HOOK *cannot even ram them down with a pole. He steals to the mouth of a tree and listens.*

Peter (*prematurely*) All is over!

Wendy But who has won?

Peter Hst! If the Indians have won they will beat the tom-tom; it is always their signal of victory.

HOOK *licks his lips at this and signs to* SMEE, *who is sitting on it, to hold up the tom-tom.* HOOK *beats upon it with his claw, and listens for results.*

Tootles The tom-tom!

Peter (*sheathing his sword*) An Indian victory! (*The cheers below are music to the black hearts above*) You are quite safe now, Wendy. Boys, goodbye. All turn your backs so as not to see your Captain cry.

He resumes his pipes. The BOYS *slowly leave their Captain, and disappear towards their holes.*

Wendy Don't forget your medicine.

She puts something into a shell and leaves it for PETER. *It is only water, but she measures it out in drops.*

Peter Oh, all right.

Wendy And don't forget to change your flannels.

Peter I won't forget.

Wendy Peter, what are you to me? You are my – what?

Peter Your son, Wendy.

Wendy Oh, goodbye!

The travellers start upon their journey little witting that HOOK *has issued his silent orders: a man to the mouth of each tree. As the* CHILDREN *squeeze up they are plucked from their trees by the* PIRATES *and trussed. The only one treated differently is* WENDY, *whom* HOOK *greets with a flamboyant bow and then escorts on his arm with dreadful politeness. As the* STORYTELLER *continues,* PETER *paces up and down the earthen floor of the underground home.*

Storyteller Unaware of the tragedy being enacted above, Peter was so full of wrath against grown-ups, who as usual were spoiling everything, that he started breathing quick short breaths at the rate of about five to a second. He did this because there is a saying in the Never Land that every time you breathe a grown-up dies; and Peter was killing them off vindictively as fast as possible.

PETER *crosses to the shell which* WENDY *has left for him, and is about to drink it when he changes his mind, putting the shell down close to the door of Slightly's tunnel.*

Storyteller Then he decided not to take his medicine, so as to grieve Wendy, and lay down on the bed, outside the coverlet, to vex her still more. Then he nearly cried; but it struck him how indignant she would be if he laughed instead; so he laughed a haughty laugh and fell asleep in the middle of it.

As PETER *laughs and falls asleep, the* STORYTELLER *moves into the underground home and sits close by the sleeping boy.*

Sometimes, though not often, he had dreams, and they were more painful than the dreams of other boys. For hours he could not be separated from these dreams, though he wailed piteously in them. At such times Wendy used to soothe him, and, when he grew calmer, put him back to bed before he quite woke up, so that he shouldn't know of the indignity to which she had subjected him. But on this occasion he had fallen at once into a dreamless sleep.

As the STORYTELLER *withdraws from the underground home,* HOOK *returns to the wood. He and* PETER *are now, as it were, alone on the island.* HOOK, *armed to the teeth, is searching noiselessly for some tree down which the nastiness of him can descend. Don't be too much alarmed by this; it is precisely the situation* PETER *would have chosen; indeed if the whole thing were pretend . . . One of his arms droops over the edge of the bed, a leg is arched, and the mouth is not so tightly closed that we cannot see the little pearls.*

HOOK *finds the tree. It is the larger one set apart for* SLIGHTLY. *Down this the pirate wiggles a passage. In the aperture below, his face emerges and goes green as he glares at the sleeping child. Does no feeling of compassion disturb his sombre breast? The man is not wholly evil. He has a thesaurus in his cabin, and is no mean performer on the flute. What really warps his mind is a presentiment that he is about to fail. This is not unconnected with a beatific smile on the face of the sleeper, whom he cannot reach owing to being stuck at the foot of the tree. He, however, sees the medicine shell within easy reach.*

Hook (*seraphically*) Medicine!

To Wendy's draught HOOK adds from a bottle five drops of poison distilled when he was weeping from the red in his eye. The expression on PETER's face merely implies that something heavenly is going on. HOOK worms his way upwards, and winding his cloak around him, as if to conceal himself from the night of which he is the blackest part, he stalks moodily towards the lagoon.

Storyteller It was gone ten o'clock by the Crocodile and Peter slept on.

From far away in the night sky a dot of light draws closer and closer, then flashes through the wood and darts down the nearest tree. It is TINKER BELL, looking for PETER, only for PETER, quite indifferent about the others when she finds him safe. She flits on to the bed and slaps him smartly on the face.

Tink Peter! Peter! Wake up, Peter!

Peter (*stirring*) Who is that?

Tink (*her words tumbling over themselves*) Peter, it's me it's me all the redskins got killed most of them and Hook and the pirates bagged the boys and Wendy too as well.

Peter The redskins were defeated?

Tink Yes!

Peter Wendy and the boys captured by the pirates!

Tink Yes!

Peter I'll rescue her, I'll rescue her!

He leaps first at his dagger, and then at his grindstone, to sharpen it. TINK *alights near the shell, and rings out a warning cry.*

Tink What's this, Peter?

Peter Oh, that is just my medicine.

Tink It's been poisoned.

Peter Poisoned? Who could have poisoned it? I promised Wendy to take it, and I will as soon as I've sharpened my dagger.

Tink No, Peter!

TINK, *who has seen its red colour and remembers the red in the pirate's eye, nobly swallows the draught just as* PETER's *hand is reaching for it.*

Peter Why, Tink, how dare you drink my medicine!

Tink Ohhh!

She flutters strangely round the room, answering him now in a very thin tinkle.

Peter What is the matter with you?

Tink It was poisoned, Peter. Hook must've poisoned it. I couldn't let you drink it.

Peter It was poisoned and you drank it to save my life! Tink, dear Tink, are you dying?

He has never called her 'dear Tink' before, and for a moment she is gay; she alights on his shoulder and gives his chin a loving bite.

Tink (*whispering*) You silly ass!

She hops over to the curtain, which slowly pulls open an inch or two as TINK *crawls inside and collapses onto her tiny bed. The boudoir, which is lit by her, flickers ominously.*

Peter Her light is growing faint. If it goes out that means she is dead.

Tink (*very faint*) If only children believed in fairies ...

Peter Tink, I can't tell what you're saying.

Tink Listen, I'm trying to tell you ... I'd get well if children believed in fairies.

Peter You'd get well if children believed in fairies? But there aren't any children here, Tink.

Tink Oh well.

Peter (*prompted by voices of protest all too near*) Perhaps there are children somewhere dreaming of the Never Land.

He stretches out his arms, to all the BOYS *and* GIRLS *of whom he is not one.*

Wherever you are, do you believe?

Some of them respond, but too few to make a difference to the brightness of TINK's *glow.*

Tink (*sitting up in bed, terribly faint now*) What do you think?

Peter (*now desperately beseeching*) Do you believe in fairies? Don't let Tink die. Say that you believe! If you believe, clap your hands.

Many clap. Some don't. A few hiss. Then perhaps there is a rush of NANAS to the nurseries to see what on earth is happening. But TINK is saved. First her voice grows strong; then she pops out of bed; then the curtain swishes open and TINK darts into the room, flashing through the underground home and then through the theatre itself more merry and impudent than ever. She doesn't think of thanking those who believed, but she would have liked to get at the ones who had hissed.

Peter (*to the BOYS and GIRLS, whom he can now see quite clearly*) Oh thank you, thank you, thank you! And now to rescue Wendy!

Tink (*outraged*) Wendy!

PETER *ascends his tree as if he were shot up it.*

Storyteller The moon was riding in a cloudy heaven when Peter rose from his tree, and set out upon his perilous quest.

Peter (*standing in the wood, his knife drawn*) Hook or me this time!

Storyteller He was frightfully happy!

ACT FIVE

SCENE ONE

The Pirate Ship

Most of the PIRATES *are carousing at present in the bowels of the ship, but on the poop* MULLINS *is visible, in the only greatcoat on the ship, raking with his glass the monstrous rocks within which the lagoon is cooped.* STARKEY *is leaning over a bulwark, silently surveying the sullen waves. He is bareheaded and is perhaps thinking with bitterness of his hat, which he sometimes sees still drifting past him with the* NEVER BIRD *sitting on it. The only sound to be heard is made by* SMEE *at his sewing machine, which lends a touch of domesticity to the night.*

HOOK *stands broodingly alone on the poop deck, the double cigar holder in his mouth. With* PETER *surely at last removed from his path we, who know how vain a tabernacle is man, would not be surprised to find him bellied out by the winds of his success, but it is not so; he is still uneasy, looking long and meaninglessly at familiar objects, such as the ship's bell or long tom, like one who may shortly be a stranger to them. It is as if Pan's terrible oath 'Hook or me this time' had already boarded the ship.*

Hook (*communing with his ego*) How still the night is; nothing sounds alive. Now is the hour when children in their homes are abed; their lips bright-browned with the good-night chocolate, and their tongues drowsily searching for belated crumbs, housed insecurely on their shining cheeks. Compare with them the children on this boat, about to, tragically, walk the plank. Split my ... infinitives, but 'tis my hour of triumph!

Clinging to this prospect he dances a few jubilant steps, but they fall below his usual form.

I should be feeling deevy, and yet a premonition of impending doom embraces me inexorably like a closing umbrella, and some disky spirit compels me now to make my dying speech, lest when dying there may be no time for it.

He sits in his sinister chair, furnished as it is with the skulls of his most celebrated victims, and adopts an attitude of melancholy heroism.

All mortals envy me, yet better perhaps for Hook to have had less ambition. Ah, 'good form', that is all that really matters. Fame, O fame, thou glittering bauble, what if the very ...

SMEE, *engrossed in his labours at the sewing machine, tears a piece of calico with a rending sound which makes the solitary* HOOK *think for a moment that the untoward has happened to his garments.*

Hook (*toying with one of the skulls*) I am the only man whom Barbecue feared, and Flint himself ... (*Another skull*) ... feared Barbecue. But, is it quite good form to be so feared by any man? Yea, more disquieting, is it not bad form even to think about good form? That is where the canker gnaws.

Another rending of the calico, and another checking of the breeches.

No little children love me. 'Tis said they find Smee

lovable. But an hour agone I found him letting the youngest of them try on his spectacles. But soft, if Smee is lovable, what can it be that makes him so?

A terrible answer presents itself.

Good form?

With a cry of rage he raises his iron hand over SMEE's *head; but he does not tear, arrested by further sudden reflection.*

To claw a man because he has good form, what would that be? Bad form! Yes, by ... carbonate of soda, yes! What if the very ...

A third rending of the calico disturbs him, and he has a private consultation with SMEE *who turns him round and evidently assures him that all is well. The peroration of his speech is nevertheless for ever lost, as eight bells strike and his* CREW *pour forth in bacchanalian orgy. From the poop he watches their dance till it frets him beyond bearing.*

Hook Quiet, you scugs, or I'll cast anchor in you!

He descends to a barrel on which there are playing cards, and his CREW *stand waiting, as ever, like whipped curs.*

Are all the prisoners bound, so that they can't fly away?

Jukes Ay, ay, Captain.

Hook Then hoist them up.

Starkey (*raising the door of the hold*) Tumble up, you ungentlemanly lubbers.

The terrified BOYS *are prodded up and from* PIRATE *to* PIRATE *tossed about the deck until they are herded into a shivering huddle at the centre of the deck.* HOOK *seems to have forgotten them; he is sitting by the barrel with his cards.*

Hook (*suddenly*) So! Now then, you bullies, six of you walk the plank tonight but I have room for two cabin-boys. Which of you is it to be?

He returns to his cards.

Tootles (*hoping to soothe him by putting the blame on the only person, vaguely remembered, who is always willing to act as a buffer*) You see, sir, I don't think my *mother* would like me to be a pirate. Would your mother like you to be a pirate, Slightly?

Slightly I don't think so, Tootles. Would your mother like you to be a pirate, Nibs?

Nibs I don't think so, Slightly. Would your mother like you to be pirates, Twins?

Twins We don't think so, Nibs. Would your . . .

Hook Stow this gab! (*To* JOHN) You boy, in the hat. You look as if you had a little pluck in you. Didst never want to be a pirate, my hearty?

John (*dazzled by being singled out*) Well, when I was at school I rather wanted to be a pirate. I thought I'd call myself Red-handed Jack.

Michael (*stepping into prominence*) What would you call me if I joined?

Hook (*for the benefit of his* CREW'*s feeble sense of humour*) Blackbeard Joe.

Michael John, what do you think?

John Stop! Should we still be respectful subjects of King Edward?

The sniggers of the CREW *swiftly die away at the mention of the forbidden subject.*

Hook (*dangerously upset*) You would have to swear 'down with King Edward!'

John (*grandly*) Then I refuse!

Michael And I refuse!

Hook That seals your doom. Bring up their mother.

WENDY *is driven up from the hold and thrown to him. She sees at the first glance that the deck has not been scrubbed for years.*

Hook So, my beauty, you are to see your children walk the plank.

Wendy (*with noble calmness*) Are they to die?

Hook They are. Silence all, for a mother's last words to her children.

Wendy These are my last words. Dear boys, I feel that I have a message to you from your real mothers, and it is this: 'We hope our sons will die like English gentlemen'.

The BOYS *go on fire.*

Tootles I am going to do what my mother hopes. What are you going to do, Slightly?

Slightly What my mother hopes. What are you going to do, Nibs?

Nibs What my mother hopes. What are you going to do, Twins?

First Twin What my mother hopes. What are you . . .

Hook (*the subject of mothers starting to grate on him*) Tie her to the mast! Get the plank ready.

The CREW *haul out the plank and bear it with ceremonial relish to the poop deck.* SMEE *is left in charge of* WENDY *for a moment and cannot resist a private plea.*

Smee (*whispering*) I'll save you if you promise to be my mother.

Wendy (*shocked and inconsiderate of* SMEE'*s finer feelings*) I'd *almost* rather have no children at all.

WENDY *is roped to the mast; but no one regards her, for all eyes are fixed upon the plank now protruding from the poop over the ship's side. A great change, however, occurs in the time* HOOK *takes to raise his claw and point to this deadly engine. No one is now looking at the plank for the tick, tick of the Crocodile is heard. Yet it is not to bear on the Crocodile that all eyes slew round, it is that they may bear on* HOOK. *Otherwise prisoners and captors are equally inert, like actors in some play who have found themselves 'on' in a scene in which they are not personally concerned. Even the iron claw hangs inactive, as if aware that the Crocodile is not coming for it. Affection for their Captain, now cowering from view, is not what has given* HOOK *his dominance over the* CREW, *but as the menacing sound draws nearer they close their eyes respectfully.*

Hook The Crocodile!

There is no Crocodile. It is PETER *who has been circling the pirate ship, ticking as he flies far more superbly than any clock. He drops into the water and climbs aboard, warning the captives with upraised finger (but still ticking) not for the moment to give audible expression to their natural admiration. Only one pirate sees him, WIBBLES of the eye patch, who comes up from below. JOHN claps a hand on WIBBLES's mouth to stifle the groan; four boys hold him to prevent the thud; PETER delivers the blow and the carrion is thrown overboard. We hear a splash.*

Slightly (*beginning to count*) One!

STARKEY is the first pirate to open his eyes, but not before PETER has slipped into the cabin. The ship seems to him to be precisely as when he closed them. He cannot interpret the sparkle that has come into the faces of the captives, who are cleverly pretending to be as afraid as ever. He little knows that the door of the dark cabin has just closed on one more boy. Indeed it is for HOOK alone he looks, and he is a little surprised to see him.

Starkey (*hoarsely*) It is gone, Captain! There is not a sound.

The tenement that is HOOK heaves tumultuously and he is himself again.

Hook (*now convinced that some fair spirit watches over him*) Then here's to Johnny Plank!

As he sings he capers detestably along an imaginary plank and his copy-cats do likewise, joining in the chorus.

Hook
    Yo ho, yo ho, the frisky plank
    You walks along it so

Till it goes down and you goes down
To tooral looral lo!

Pirates

Yo ho, yo ho, the frisky plank
You walks along it so . . .

The brave CHILDREN *try to stem this monstrous torrent by breaking into the national anthem.*

Children

God save our gracious King
Long live our noble King
God save the King . . .

The PIRATES *redouble their efforts . . .*

Pirates

. . . Till it goes down and you goes down
To tooral looral lo!

. . . but the CHILDREN *are not to be deflected.*

Children

. . . Send him victorious, happy and glorious
Long to reign over us
God save the King!

The CHILDREN'*s voices hang in the air, causing patriotic unease in even the most treacherous of hearts.*

Starkey (*paling*) I don't like it, messmates!

Hook Stow that, Starkey!

Unhappy to be bested by a choir of CHILDREN, HOOK *sings back at them with a vengeance . . .*

Yo ho, yo ho, the frisky plank . . .

... but then a much nastier riposte occurs to him.

Tell me, boys, do you want a touch of the cat before you walk the plank?

He is more pitiless than ever now that he believes he has a charmed life.

Fetch the cat o' nine tails, Jukes; it is in the cabin.

Jukes Ay, ay, sir.

It is one of his commonest remarks, and it is only recorded now because he never makes another. The stage direction 'Exit JUKES' has in this case a special significance. But only the CHILDREN *know that someone is awaiting this unfortunate in the cabin, and* HOOK *tramples them down as he resumes his ditty.*

Hook

Yo ho, yo ho, the scratching cat
Its tails are nine you know,
And when they're writ upon your back,
You're fit to ...

The last words will ever remain a matter for conjecture, for from the dark cabin comes a curdling screech which wails through the ship and dies away. It is followed by a sound, almost more eerie in the circumstances, that can only be likened to the crowing of a cock.

Hook What was that?

Slightly (*solemnly*) Two!

Hook Cecco.

CECCO *swings into the cabin, and in a moment returns, livid.*

Hook (*with an effort*) What is the matter with Bill Jukes, you dog?

Cecco The matter with him is he is dead – stabbed.

Mullins Bill Jukes' dead!

Cecco The cabin is as black as a pit, but there is something terrible in there: the thing you heard a-doodle-dooing.

Hook (*slowly*) Cecco, go back and fetch me out that doodle-doo.

Cecco (*unstrung*) No, Captain, no.

He supplicates on his knees, but his master advances on him implacably.

Hook (*in his most syrupy voice*) Did you say you would go, Cecco?

CECCO *goes. All listen. There is one screech, one crow.*

Slightly (*as if he were a bell tolling*) Three!

Hook 'Sdeath and oddfish, who is to bring me out that doodle-doo?

No one steps forward.

Starkey (*injudiciously, the black looks of some others encouraging him*) Wait till Cecco comes out.

Hook I think I heard you volunteer, Starkey.

Starkey (*emphatically*) No, by thunder!

Hook (*with those lyrical tones which might be more engaging when accompanied by his flute*) My hook thinks you did. I wonder if it would not be advisable, Starkey, to humour the hook?

Starkey I'll swing before I go in there.

Hook (*gleaming*) Is it mutiny? Starkey is ringleader. Shake hands, Starkey.

STARKEY *recoils from the hook. It follows him till he leaps overboard.*

Slightly Four!

Hook (*genially, to the remaining crew*) Did any other gentleman say mutiny?

They indicate that they did not even know the late STAR-KEY.

I will bring out that doodle-doo myself.

He raises a blunderbuss but casts it from him with a menacing gesture which means that he has more faith in the claw. With a lighted lantern in his hand he enters the cabin. Not a sound is to be heard now on the ship, unless it be SLIGHTLY *wetting his lips to say 'five'.* HOOK *staggers out.*

(*Unsteadily*) Something blew out the light.

Mullins (*with dark meaning*) Some – *thing?*

Noodler What of Cecco?

Hook He is dead as Jukes.

They are superstitious like all sailors, and MULLINS *has planted a dire conception in their minds.*

Cookson They do say as the surest sign a ship's accurst is when there is one aboard more than can be accounted for.

Noodler I've heard he allus boards the pirate craft at last. (*With a dreadful significance*) Has he a tail, Captain?

Mullins They say that when he comes it is in the likeness of the wickedest man aboard.

Cookson (*clinching it*) Has he a hook, Captain?

Knives and pistols come to hand, and there is a general cry –

Pirates The ship is doomed!

– but it is not his dogs that can frighten JAS. HOOK. *Hearing something like a cheer from the* BOYS *he wheels round, and his face brings them to their knees.*

Hook So you like it, do you? (*Turning back to his* CREW) By Caius and Balbus, bullies, here is a notion: open the cabin door and drive them in. Let them fight the doodle-doo for their lives. If they kill him we are so much the better; if he kills them we are none the worse.

This masterly stroke restores their confidence; and the BOYS, *affecting fear, are driven into the cabin. Once out of sight they give vent to a bloodcurdling cacophony of screams. Desperadoes though the* PIRATES *are, some of them have been boys themselves, and all turn their backs to the cabin and listen, with arms outstretched to it as if to ward off the horrors that are being enacted there.*

Inside the cabin PETER *relieves the* BOYS *of their manacles, and steals softly as a snowflake out of the cabin and on to the poop. The screams continue from the cabin as he releases* WENDY; *and now it would be easy for them all to fly away, but it is to be* HOOK *or him this time. He signs to her to hide, and with awful grimness folding her cloak around him, the hood over his head, he takes her place by the mast. The screams subside into a deathly silence.* PETER *crows.*

Mullins The doodle-doo has killed them all!

Several Pirates The ship's bewitched.

They advance on HOOK, *every blade aimed at his throat.*

Hook I've thought it out, lads; there is a Jonah aboard.

Cookson (*snapping at him*) Ay, a man with a hook.

If he were to withdraw one step their knives would be in him, but he does not flinch.

Hook (*temporizing*) No, lads, no, it is the girl. Never was luck on a pirate ship wi' a woman aboard. We'll right the ship when she has gone.

Mullins (*lowering his cutlass*) It's worth trying.

Hook Throw the girl overboard.

Mullins (*jeering*) There is none can save you now, missy.

Wendy (*from behind the mast*) There is one!

Mullins Who is that?

Peter (*casting off the cloak*) Peter Pan, the avenger!

Hook (*throwing out a suggestion*) Cleave him to the brisket.

Peter Up, boys, and at them!

Armed with such weapons as they can lay their hands on the BOYS *leap from their concealment in the cabin, and the clash of arms resounds through the vessel. Man to man the* PIRATES *are the stronger, but they are unnerved by the suddenness of the onslaught and they scatter, thus enabling their opponents to hunt in couples and choose their quarry. Some are hurled into the lagoon; others are dragged from dark recesses. There is no boy whose weapon is not reeking save* SLIGHTLY, *who runs about with a lantern, counting, ever counting.*

Wendy (*meeting with* MICHAEL *in a moment's lull*) Oh, Michael, stay with me, protect me!

Michael (*reeling*) Wendy, I've killed a pirate!

Wendy It's awful, awful.

Michael No, it isn't, I like it, I like it.

He casts himself into the fray once more, as does WENDY. *One by one the* PIRATES *are despatched, until only* HOOK *is left.*

Slightly Twenty!

The BOYS *encircle* HOOK. *Again and again they close upon him and again and again he hews a clear space.*

Hook Back, back, you mice. It's Hook; do you like him?

He lifts up MICHAEL *with his claw and uses him as a buckler. A terrible voice breaks in.*

Peter Put up your swords, boys. This man is mine.

HOOK *shakes* MICHAEL *off his claw as if he were a drop of water, and these two antagonists face each other for their final bout. They measure swords at arms' length, make a sweeping motion with them, and bringing the points to the deck, rest their hands upon the hilts.*

Hook (*with curling lip*) So, Pan, this is all your doing!

Peter Ay, James Hook, it is all my doing.

Hook Proud and insolent youth, prepare to meet thy doom!

Peter Dark and canister man . . .

Tootles (*prompting*) Sinister!

Peter ... sinister man. Have at thee!

HOOK *or* PETER *this time! They fall to without another word.* PETER *is a rare swordsman, and parries with dazzling rapidity, sometimes before the other can make his stroke.* HOOK, *if not quite so nimble in wrist play, has the advantage of a yard or two in reach, but though they close he cannot give the quietus with his claw, which seems to find nothing to tear at. He does not, especially in the most heated moments, quite see* PETER, *who to his eyes, now blurred or opened clearly for the first time, is less like a boy than a mote of dust dancing in the sun. By some impalpable stroke* HOOK's *sword is whipped from his grasp, and when he stoops to raise it a little foot is on its blade. There is no deep gash on* HOOK, *but he is suffering torment as from innumerable jags.*

Children (*exulting*) Now, Peter, now!

PETER *raises the sword by its blade, and with an inclination of the head that is perhaps slightly overdone, presents the hilt to his enemy.*

Children Good form!

Hook (*stung to madness*) To't again!

He now has a damp feeling that this boy is the weapon which is to strike him from the lists of man; but the grandeur of his mind still holds and, true to the traditions of his flag, he fights on like a human flail. PETER *flutters round and through and over these gyrations as if the wind of them blew him out of the danger zone, and again and again he darts in and jags. Infuriated,* HOOK *drives* PETER *up the rigging into the crow's nest, though perhaps* PETER, *sensing too easy a victory, has allowed himself to be driven there.*

Hook 'Tis some fiend fighting me. Pan, who and what art thou?

The CHILDREN *listen eagerly for the answer, none quite so eagerly as* WENDY.

Peter (*at a venture*) I'm youth, I'm joy . . .

PETER *flies from the crow's nest.*

. . . I'm a little bird that has broken out of the egg!

The CHILDREN *cheer but not for long.*

Hook Death to you all! I'll fire the powder magazine.

He disappears, they know not where.

Children Peter, save us!

HOOK *returns, with a smoking bomb in his hand.*

Hook (*with gloomy satisfaction*) If I am to die, you all die with me. In thirty seconds the ship will be blown to smithereens.

He reclines in his chair, nursing the bomb, while the CHILDREN *cast themselves before him in entreaty.*

Children Mercy! Mercy!

Hook (*taunting them with the bomb*) Back, you pewling spawn! I'll show you now the road to dusty death! (*The idea lighting up his doomed visage*) A holocaust of children, there is something grand in the idea!

HOOK *closes his eyes in preparation for the blast.* PETER *flies over to the chair, plucks off one of the Captain's treasured skull-trophies and deftly swaps it with the bomb in* HOOK's *hand. When* HOOK *next opens his eyes, his first sight*

is the skull of Barbecue grinning up at him, his second the boy
PETER *casually tossing the bomb overboard. It explodes. The
children cheer but the desperate and exasperated* HOOK *has
one more card to play. He turns one of the ship's cannons
towards* WENDY *and the* BOYS *and loads it with a
cannonball.* PETER *lands back on the deck and bravely
positions himself in front of the terrified* CHILDREN,
preparing to protect them from the blast. HOOK *lights the
fuse and there is a deafening roar as the cannon fires.* PETER
*is hit by the cannonball amidships and is driven backwards
across the deck by the force of it.* HOOK *is exultant but his
victory freezes on his face as* PETER, *regaining his balance,
holds up the cannonball in triumph. Alas, it is still hot from the
cannon and he juggles it for a moment as you would a hot
potato straight from the oven before tossing it to* SLIGHTLY,
*who drops to the deck under its weight. At the sight of all this
tomfoolery the great heart of* HOOK *breaks.*

Children
> Yo ho, yo ho, the frisky plank
> You walks along it so
> Till it goes down and you goes down
> To Davy Jones below!

As the children sing their mocking refrain, HOOK *climbs the
bulwarks and prostrates himself into the water, where the*
CROCODILE *is waiting for him, open-mouthed.* HOOK
*knows the purpose of this yawning cavity, but after what he
has been through he enters it like one greeting a friend.*

Hook (*in the mouth of the* CROCODILE) Peter Pan, no
words of mine can express my utter contempt for you.

Peter (*from high up on the poop*) James Hook, thou not
wholly unheroic figure, farewell.

Hook (*disappearing from view*) Floreat Etona!

PETER *descends to the main deck and puts on* HOOK's *discarded coat as the* STORYTELLER *appears at the side of the stage.*

Storyteller For the children the lateness of the hour was almost the biggest thing of all. Wendy got them to bed in the pirates' bunks pretty quickly you may be sure ...

PETER *crosses the deck, a very Napoleon, and sits himself down in* HOOK's *great chair, glaring at the other* CHILDREN, *one finger crooked in the shape of a hook.*

Storyteller ... all but Captain Pan who strutted up and down on deck until at last he fell asleep under the stars.

As the CHILDREN *exit to the cabin,* WENDY *joins* PETER *in the Captain's chair and holds him as he sleeps.*

He had one of his dreams that night and cried in his sleep for a long time, and Wendy held him tight.

The ship, and PETER *and* WENDY *disappear from view.*

By two bells that morning they were all stirring their stumps, for there was a big sea running. They all donned pirate clothes, cut off at the knee, shaved smartly, and tumbled up, chewing tobacco.

Captain Pan calculated that if this weather lasted they should strike the Azores about the twenty-first of June, after which it would save time to fly. We must arrive in England before these rubbishy children, so there's no time to lose ...

Music, as the STORYTELLER *dons flying helmet and goggles and takes to the air.*

As we leave these magic shores we can still just hear the sound of the surf and far below us the mermaids singing in the dark lagoon.

The NEVER OSTRICH *appears below him and stalks slowly across the stage.*

The beasts are still out looking for the redskins, but the redskins are departing now, in search of happier hunting-grounds.

The STORYTELLER *flies up and away as* TIGER LILY *and* GREAT BIG LITTLE PANTHER *appear with a remnant of the* TRIBE. *Bringing up the rear of the Indian file is* STARKEY, *laden with papooses.* SMEE *appears from another direction, wringing sea-water from his hat.*

Smee You, Starkey.

Starkey (*detaching himself from the tribe*) It's me, Smee.

Smee I thought you were drowned.

Starkey No, Smee, I was captured by the redskins. The squaws make me carry their babies.

Smee It's a comedown for a pirate.

Starkey I shall become vulgar.

Smee Never. (*Taking one of the papooses from* STARKEY) Oh, surely, never.

Starkey What a go is life.

Smee (*resisting the temptation to dandle*) But always interesting.

Starkey What was the Captain's fate?

Smee I know not. I saw the Crocodile following him. But I'm not sure whether it got him.

Enter CROCODILE. STARKEY *starts away in fear.*

Have no fear, Starkey.

He offers it an arm and a leg. The CROCODILE *despises them.*

He only eats swells.

Starkey (*calling into the* CROCODILE*'s mouth*) Captain? Are you there?

Both Captain?!

The CROCODILE *gives vent to a stentorian belch and vomits the hook.*

Smee (*picking up the hook*) It has got him. O Tempora! O Morris!

Solemn music. As SMEE *and* STARKEY *sing a brief salute to their departed master, the* CROCODILE *plods away like one who has lived his great hour and can afford to take the rest of his life more leisurely.*

Smee/Starkey
> Oh, Captain Hook
> The greatest pirate on the seven seas
> The terror of the ocean wide
> May he rest in peace.

TIGER LILY *returns from offstage with one or two other* SQUAWS.

Tiger Lily (*glaring at* Smee *and* Starkey) Starkey!

Squaws Come, Starkey! Starkey, bring babies!

Starkey Load me up wi' that papoose, will you, Smee.

SMEE *returns the papoose to* STARKEY.

Smee (*loading*) There you go.

Starkey Goodbye, Smee, thou plebeian but honest heart, goodbye.

Smee So long, Starkey, thou gentlemanly character, farewell.

They depart in opposite directions, STARKEY *hurrying after* TIGER LILY *and the* SQUAWS, *and* SMEE *more thoughtfully, his Captain's hook in his hand. Indeed, from that day forth,* SMEE *wandered about the world in his spectacles, making a precarious living by saying he was the only man that James Hook had feared.*

SCENE TWO

The Nursery

The old nursery appears again with everything as it was at the beginning of the play, except that the kennel has gone and the window is standing open. So Peter was wrong about mothers; indeed there is no subject upon which he is so likely to be wrong.

Storyteller We are now returning to that desolate home from which Wendy, John and Michael had taken heartless flight so long ago. Would it not serve them jolly well right if they came back and found that their parents were spending the weekend in the country? It would be the moral lesson they have been in need of ever since we met them!

MRS DARLING *is asleep on a chair near the window, her eyes tired with searching the heavens.* NANA *is stretched out listless on the floor. She is the cynical one, and though custom has made her hang the children's night things on the fireguard for an airing, she surveys them not hopefully, but with some self-contempt.*

Mrs Darling (*starting up as if we had whispered to her that her brats are coming back*) Wendy! John! Michael!

NANA *lifts a sympathetic paw to the poor soul's lap.*

Mrs Darling Oh, Nana, it is only a dream! I dreamt my children had come back! You have put their night things out again! Nana, it has touched my heart to see you do that night after night, as if you expected my children to come back, but they will never come back!

In trouble the difference of station can be completely ignored, and it is not strange to see these two using the same handkerchief. Enter LIZA, *who in the gentleness with which the house has been run of late, is perhaps a little more masterful than of yore.*

Liza (*feeling herself degraded by the announcement*) Nana's dinner is served.

NANA, *who quite understands what are* LIZA's *feelings, departs for the dining-room with our exasperating leisureliness, instead of running, as we would all do if we followed our instincts.*

Mrs Darling Is the master's own dinner ready yet, Liza?

Liza Yes, it's here.

She places a rather handsome dog bowl on the floor, together with a napkin and a knife and fork.

(*Bursting forth*) I want to give notice!

Mrs Darling (*pained*) Oh, Liza, is it the stairs?

Liza No, ma'am, it's the master. To think I have a master as have changed places with his dog!

Mrs Darling (*gently*) Out of remorse, Liza.

Interested cheers from the street.

Liza That is the cab fetching him back. I don't think it's respectable to go to his office in a kennel, with the street-boys running alongside cheering.

Even this does not arouse her mistress, which may have been the honourable intention. The kennel is conveyed to its old place by a CABBY *and* FRIEND, *and* MR DARLING *scrambles out of it in his office clothes.*

Mr Darling Thank you, my men. (*Giving* LIZA *his hat loftily*) If you will be so good, Liza.

The cheering is resumed.

It is very gratifying.

Liza (*contemptuous*) Lot of little boys.

Mr Darling (*with the new sweetness of one who has sworn never to lose his temper again*) There were several adults today.

She goes off scornfully with the hat and the TWO MEN, *but he has not a word of reproach for her. It ought to melt us when we see how humbly grateful he is for a kiss from his wife, so much more than he feels he deserves. One may think he is wrong to exchange into the kennel, but sorrow has taught him that he is the kind of man who whatever he does contritely he must do to excess; otherwise he abandons doing it.*

Mrs Darling (*who has known this for quite a long time*) What sort of day have you had, George?

He is sitting on the floor by the kennel.

Mr Darling There were never less than a hundred running around the cab cheering, and when we passed the Stock Exchange the members came out and waved.

He is exultant but uncertain of himself, and with a word she could dispirit him utterly.

Mrs Darling (*bravely*) I am so proud, George.

Mr Darling (*commendation from the dearest quarter ever going to his head*) I have been put on a picture postcard, dear.

Mrs Darling (*nobly*) Never!

Mr Darling And I've had six invitations to dinner from leaders of society.

Mrs Darling All asking you to come in your kennel?

Mr Darling (*thoughtlessly*) Ah, Mary, we should not be such celebrities if the children hadn't flown away.

Mrs Darling (*startled*) George, you are sure you are not enjoying it?

Mr Darling (*anxiously*) Enjoying it! See my punishment, living in a kennel.

Mrs Darling Forgive me, dear one.

Mr Darling It is I who need forgiveness, always I, never you. And now I feel drowsy.

He retires into the kennel.

Won't you play me to sleep on the drawing-room piano? And shut that window, Mary dearest; I feel a draught.

Mrs Darling Oh, George, never ask me to do that. The window must always be left open for them, always, always.

MRS DARLING *moves from bed to bed lighting the night-lights and crooning a lullaby just as she did on that fateful night so long ago.*

In the quiet of the night
May the wanderers see a light
That will lead them safely on
To the shelter of their home
And with all their perils past
May they reach their home at last.

She turns down the gas, and quietly crying, she leaves the nursery to play her husband to sleep on the drawing-room piano.

The truants alight on the sill, and enter the darkened room. JOHN to his credit having the tired MICHAEL on his shoulders. They have nothing else to their credit; no compunction for what they have done, not the tiniest fear that any just person may be awaiting them with a stick. The youngest is in a daze, but the two others are shining virtuously like holy people who are about to give two other people a treat.

Michael (*looking about him*) I think I have been here before.

John It's your home, you stupid.

Wendy There is your old bed, Michael.

Michael I had nearly forgotten.

John I say, the kennel!

Wendy Perhaps Nana is in it.

John (*peering*) There is a man asleep in it.

Wendy (*remembering him by his bald patch*) It's Father!

John So it is!

Michael Let me see Father. (*Disappointed*) He is not as big as the pirate I killed.

John (*perplexed*) Wendy, surely Father didn't use to sleep in the kennel?

Wendy (*with misgivings*) Perhaps we don't remember the old life as well as we thought we did.

John (*chilled*) It is very careless of Mother not to be here when we come back.

The piano is heard.

Wendy H'sh! (*She goes to the door and peeps*) That is her playing!

They all have a peep.

Michael Who is that lady?

John H'sh! It's Mother.

Michael Then are you not really our mother, Wendy?

Wendy (*with conviction*) Oh dear, it is quite time to be back!

John Let us creep in and put our hands over her eyes.

Wendy (*more considerate*) No, let us break it to her gently.

She slips between the sheets of her bed; and the others, seeing the idea at once, get into their beds. Then when the music stops they cover their heads. There are now three distinct bumps in the beds. MRS DARLING *sees the bumps as soon as she comes in, but she does not believe she sees them.*

Mrs Darling I see them in their beds so often in my dreams that I seem still to see them when I am awake.

She sits down and turns away her face from the bumps, though of course they are still reflected in her mind.

So often their silver voices call me, my little children whom I'll see no more.

Silver voices is a good one, especially about John; but the heads pop up.

Wendy (*perhaps rather silvery*) Mother!

Mrs Darling (*without moving*) That is Wendy.

John (*quite gruff*) Mother!

Mrs Darling Now it is John.

Michael (*no better than a squeak*) Mother!

Mrs Darling Now Michael. And when they call I stretch out my arms to them, but they never come, they never come!

She stretches out her arms for the three little selfish children they would never envelop again. Yes, they did, they went round WENDY *and* JOHN *and* MICHAEL, *who had slipped out of their beds and run to her.*

Mrs Darling George! George!

MR DARLING *wakes to share her bliss.* NANA *comes rushing in, and* LIZA, *to greet the homecomers.*

Tootles (*appearing at the window*) Wendy, we can't hold on to the rain spout any longer.

Wendy Come in, boys.

Mrs Darling (*startled*) Why, who ... what ...

Wendy It's all right, Mummy, they're just a few motherless boys we've brought back with us.

Mrs Darling But, my love ...

All come in, hats in hand and carrying their bundles. They stand timidly in a respectful row.

Wendy Oh, Mummy, say you'll have them!

Mrs Darling Of course I will!

Mr Darling (*to* WENDY) I must say, Wendy, that you don't do things by halves.

Tootles Do you think we should be too much of a handful, sir? Because if so we can go away.

Wendy Father!

Nibs We could sleep doubled up.

Wendy I always cut their hair myself.

Mrs Darling George!

Mr Darling (*bursting into tears*) I'm as glad to have them as you are, but they should have asked my consent as well as yours, instead of treating me as a cypher in my own house.

All the BOYS *gather round* MR DARLING, *only* SLIGHTLY *holding back.*

Tootles I don't think he's a cypher. Do you think he's a cypher, Curly?

Curly No, I don't. Do you think he's a cypher, Nibs?

Nibs No, I don't. Do you think he's a cypher, Twins?

Twins No, we don't. Do you think he is a cypher, Slightly?

Although gratified, MR DARLING *is strangely irritated by these repetitious remarks.*

Mr Darling Stow that gab! ... (*Regaining his composure*) I'm sorry ... I dare say we could find space for you all in the drawing-room, if you can be fitted in.

Tootles We'll fit in, sir.

Mr Darling Then follow the leader. Mind you, I'm not sure that we have a drawing-room, but we *pretend* we have, and it's all the same. Hoop-la!

Boys Hoop-la!

He dances out of the room and they all dance after him, save SLIGHTLY *who remains behind, somewhat troubled.*

Liza What is the matter, boy?

Slightly My mother doesn't seem to be here.

Liza (*starting back*) Is your name Slightly?

Slightly Yes'm.

Liza Would that be 'Slightly Soiled'?

Slightly (*amazed*) Yes.

Liza Then *I* am your mother!

Slightly How do you know?

Liza (*the good-natured creature*) I feel it in my bones.

They go into the house and there is none happier now than SLIGHTLY, *unless it be* NANA *who follows them out with the importance of a nurse who will never have another day off.* MRS DARLING *is now alone in the nursery with her* THREE CHILDREN *as the* STORYTELLER *reappears.*

Storyteller There could not have been a simpler, happier family than the Darling family that night ...

Mrs Darling (*holding them closer than close*) My Darlings!

PETER's *face appears at the window.*

Storyteller ... but there was none to see them except a strange boy who was staring in at the window. He had ecstasies innumerable that other children can never know; but he was looking through the window at the one joy from which he must be for ever barred.

Boys (*calling excitedly from downstairs*) John, Michael!

JOHN *and* MICHAEL *run to join their friends without a second glance at their happy mother.* WENDY *suddenly sees* PETER *at the window.*

Wendy Peter!

She runs to the window and lets PETER *in. He sits on the window ledge for a moment and then warily circles the room, keeping* MRS DARLING *at a safe distance.*

Storyteller Mrs Darling was the loveliest age for a woman, but too old to see Peter clearly.

Mrs Darling Peter, where are you? Let me adopt you too.

Peter (*perching on the end of Wendy's bed*) Would you send me to school?

Mrs Darling (*obligingly*) Yes.

Peter And then to an office?

Mrs darling I suppose so.

Peter Soon I should be a man?

Mrs Darling (*reaching out her arms to the lost child*) Very soon.

Peter (*passionately*) Hands off, lady! I don't want to go to school and learn solemn things. No one is going to catch me, lady, and make me a man. I want always to be a boy and to have fun.

So perhaps he thinks, but it is only his greatest pretend.

Wendy You will be rather lonely in the evenings, Peter!

Peter (*rather hurtfully*) I shall have Tink.

Wendy Oh, Peter! Tink can't go a twentieth part of the way round! Mother, may I go?

Mrs Darling (*gripping her for ever*) Certainly not. I have got you home again, and I mean to keep you.

Wendy But he does so need a mother.

Mrs Darling So do you, my love, so do you. (WENDY *nods, just a little reluctantly, but with a good grace*) But, Peter, I shall let her go to you once a year for a week to do your spring-cleaning.

WENDY *revels in this, but* PETER, *who has no notion what a spring-cleaning is, waves a rather careless thanks.*

Mrs Darling Say good night, Wendy.

Wendy Good night, Peter.

Peter Good night, Wendy.

MRS DARLING *is a little startled to feel a light touch on her cheek as* PETER *passes her on his way to the window.*

Wendy (*calling through the window after him*) Peter! You won't forget me, will you, before next spring-cleaning time comes?

Storyteller Of course Peter promised; and then he flew away. He took Mrs Darling's kiss with him. That kiss, which had been for no one else, Peter took quite easily.

MRS DARLING *smiles to herself...*

Storyteller Funny. But she seemed satisfied.

... and leaves the nursery, which darkens as she goes.

Of course all the boys went to school; it is sad to say that the power to fly gradually left them. Want of practice they called it, but what it really meant was that they no longer believed. Michael went on believing in him longer than the other boys, though they jeered at him; so he was with Wendy when Peter came for her at the end of the first year. She flew away with Peter in the frock she had woven from leaves and berries in the Never Land, and he was exactly as fascinating as ever. But the week was over, oh, so quickly.

WENDY *and* PETER *are huddled together on the floor of the nursery.* MICHAEL *is sitting on the end of his bed.*

Wendy Remember not to bite your nails.

Peter All right!

Wendy When you come for me next year, Peter ... you will come, won't you?

Peter Yes. (*Gloating*) To hear stories about me!

Wendy It is so queer that the stories you like best should be the ones about yourself.

Peter (*touchy*) Well then?

Wendy (*waxing sentimental*) Peter, I want to tell you something.

Peter (*enthralled*) Is it a secret?

Wendy Oh, Peter! When Captain Hook carried us away ...

Peter (*interrupting, wide-eyed*) Who's Captain Hook? Is it a story? Tell it me!

Wendy Do you mean to say you've forgotten Captain Hook? And how you killed him and saved all our lives?

Peter I forget them after I kill them.

Wendy (*wondering about her rival*) I didn't see Tink this time.

Peter Who?

Wendy Tinker Bell! Your fairy!

Peter (*carelessly*) There are such a lot of them. I expect she is no more.

Wendy (*pained*) Oh, Peter, you forget everything.

Peter Everything except Mother Wendy.

The nursery darkens once more and the STORYTELLER *comes back into view.*

Storyteller But next year he did forget. She waited in a new frock because the old one simply would not meet; but he never came.

We see WENDY *huddled at the end of her bed, her eiderdown wrapped tightly around her.* MICHAEL *is gazing forlornly out of the open window.*

Michael Perhaps he's ill.

Wendy You know he is never ill.

MICHAEL *closes the window, and turns to* WENDY.

Michael Perhaps there is no such person, Wendy.

MICHAEL *starts to cry and goes to* WENDY *for comfort.*

Storyteller And then Wendy would have cried if Michael had not been crying.

The nursery darkens once more and disappears from view.

Peter came next spring-cleaning; and the strange thing was that he never knew he had missed a year. But that was the last time the girl Wendy saw him. She tried not to have growing pains and she felt untrue to him when she won a prize for general knowledge. But the years came and went without bringing the careless boy and Wendy – grew – up. You need not be sorry for her. She was one of the kind that likes to grow up. All of the boys were grown up and done for by this time; so it is scarcely worth while saying anything about them.

As they are named the GROWN-UP BOYS *cross the stage in adult attire.*

You may see the Twins, and Nibs every day going to an office, each carrying a little bag and an umbrella. Curly is up at Oxford. Slightly married a lady of title and so he became a lord. You see that judge in a wig coming out of the iron door? That used to be Tootles. Michael is an engine driver. The bearded man who doesn't know any stories to tell his children was once John.

The GROWN-UP BOYS *disappear into the darkness and the nursery begins to creep back into view.*

Years rolled on again, and Wendy had a daughter. (*This ought not to be written in ink but in a golden splash*) She was called Jane, and when she was old enough to ask questions they were mostly about Peter Pan, and Wendy told her all she could remember in the very nursery from which the famous flight had taken place.

We can now see the nursery clearly. The kennel has disappeared as has one of the beds and there is an electric light in place of the old gas light fitting of previous years. JANE *can be seen asleep in* WENDY's *old bed, very like* WENDY *used to look when she was* JANE's *age.*

And then one night came the tragedy. It was the spring of the year, and the story had been told for the night, and Jane was now asleep in her bed.

WENDY *comes into the nursery. She is a beautiful woman of about thirty or so and is rather grandly dressed for dinner in a fashionable gown of the 1920s. She goes over to* JANE's *bed to light the night-light, and she is startled by a strange little face at the window and a hand groping as if it wanted to come in.*

Wendy Peter!

The window blows open, as of old, and PETER *drops to the floor.* WENDY, *helpless and guilty, squeezes herself as small as possible, something inside of her crying, 'Woman, woman, let go of me.'*

Peter Hullo, Wendy.

Wendy (*faintly*) Hullo, Peter.

Peter (*missing the third bed*) Hullo! Where is John?

Wendy John ... doesn't sleep here now.

Peter (*with a careless glance at* JANE) Is Michael asleep?

Wendy (*hesitating*) Yes. (*Horrified at herself*) That isn't Michael.

Peter (*looking more closely*) Hullo, is it a new one?

Wendy Yes.

Peter Boy or girl?

Wendy Girl.

Peter Do you like her?

Wendy Yes. (*Faltering*) Peter ... are you expecting me to fly away with you?

Peter Of course, that is why I've come. (*A little sternly*) Have you forgotten that this is spring-cleaning time? Come on. I'm Captain!

Wendy I can't come. I've forgotten how to fly.

Peter (*taking her by the hand*) I'll soon teach you again.

Wendy Oh, Peter, don't waste the fairy dust on me.

Silently she lets her hand play with his hair and caresses his face smiling through her tears.

Peter (*a fear at last assailing him*) What is it?

Wendy I will turn on the light and then you can see for yourself.

Peter (*frightened – husky*) Wendy, don't turn on the light.

She crosses to the doorway, switches on the electric light and turns to face him. A bewildered understanding starts to come to him.

Peter What is it? What is it?

Wendy I am old, Peter. I am ever so much more than twenty. I grew up long ago.

Peter You promised not to!

Wendy I couldn't help it. I am a married woman, Peter.

Peter No, you're not.

Wendy Yes, and the little girl in the bed is my baby.

Peter No she's not. (*After a pause – fiercely*) What does she call you?

Wendy Mother.

Peter (*desolate*) Mother?

Wendy Oh, Peter, Peter!

She knows not what to do, and rushes from the room in agony. PETER takes a step towards the sleeping CHILD, with a little dagger in his hand upraised, then is about to fly away, then flings himself on the floor and sobs. JANE wakes up.

Jane Boy, why are you crying?

PETER *jumps up, and crossing to the foot of the bed, bows to her in the fairy way, exactly as he did on that first occasion when he came back for his shadow.* JANE, *impressed, bows to him from the bed.*

Peter Hullo.

Jane Hullo.

Peter My name is Peter Pan.

Jane (*simply*) Yes, I know.

Peter I came for my mother to take her to the Never Land to do my spring-cleaning.

Jane Yes, I know. I've been waiting for you.

Peter Will *you* be my mother?

Jane Oh yes.

JANE *descends from the bed and stands by* PETER's *side, with the look on her face that he likes to see on ladies when they gaze at him.* WENDY *has returned to the room and is looking at them ruefully.*

Peter And you'll come with me?

Jane If Mummy says I may.

Wendy Oh!

Jane He does so need a mother.

Wendy (*rather forlornly*) Yes, I know.

Jane May I, Mummy?

Wendy (*sighing*) May I come too?

Peter (*with more than a hint of revenge*) You can't fly!

Wendy Oh, Peter, how I wish I could take you up and squdge you! (*He draws back*) Yes, I know.

Storyteller In a sort of way he knows what she means by 'yes, I know', but in most sorts of ways he doesn't. It has something to do with the riddle of his existence. If he could get the hang of it his cry might become 'To *live* would be an awfully big adventure!' but he can never get the hang of it. Of course in the end Wendy let them fly away together, to the Never Land.

PETER *and* JANE *fly out of the nursery window.*

Peter (*shouting – gleeful*) Second to the right and then straight on till morning!

Storyteller Our last glimpse of Wendy shows her at the window, watching them receding into the sky until they were as small as stars.

Wendy (*her hands reaching out, calling with her all might*) Peter!

The nursery and the house and WENDY *begin to disappear . . .*

Storyteller As you look at Wendy you may see her hair becoming white and her figure little again, for all this happened long ago.

. . . and are gone.

Jane became a common grown-up with a daughter called Margaret; and every spring-cleaning time, except when he forgot, Peter came for Margaret and took her to the Never Land, where she told him stories about himself, to which he listened eagerly.

When Margaret grew up she had a daughter who was Peter's mother in turn, and she will have a daughter too, and thus it will go on, so long as children are young, and innocent ... and heartless!

Will you dream now of the Never Land in years to come?

We see PETER, *flying high above us. He produces his pipes and starts to play.*

He plays on and on and on ... till we *wake up*!

The end.

Breinigsville, PA USA
04 October 2010

246683BV00004B/2/P